THAT YOU MAY KNOW

A 40-Day Devotional Exploring the Life

of Jesus from the Gospel of Luke

PETER DEHAAN

ISBN:
>   978-1-948082-76-1 (ebook)
>   978-1-948082-77-8 (paperback)
>   978-1-948082-78-5 (hardcover)

Library of Congress Control Number: 2021920598

Published by Rock Rooster Books, Grand Rapids, Michigan

Credits:
>   Developmental editor: Cathy Rueter
>   Copy editor/proofreader: Robyn Mulder
>   Cover design: Taryn Nergaard
>   Author photo: Chelsie Jensen Photography

To Laura Alexander

Books in the Dear Theophilus series

The Dear Theophilus series of devotional Bible studies:

That You May Know (the gospel of Luke)

Tongues of Fire (the book of Acts)

For Unto Us (the prophet Isaiah)

Return to Me (the Minor Prophets)

I Hope in Him (the book of Job)

Living Water (the gospel of John)

Love Is Patient (Paul's letters to the Corinthians)

Be the first to hear about Peter's new books and receive monthly updates when you sign up at https://www.peterdehaan.com/updates/.

Contents

Let's Get Started

Many people skip the introduction in books, but to get the most from this one, the next part is important. I'll keep it short.

Here's what I want to share:

- Whenever you see quotation marks in the text, it's dialogue, not quoted Scripture.

- All dialogue is a paraphrase of what the speakers said or my thoughts of what they may have said.

- I use the Bible to study the Bible and avoid consulting secondary sources. Mostly, I use the NIV, but I'm open to any version that gives clarity. Of course, the Holy Spirit guides me as I study.

The book of Luke is amazing. I couldn't cover everything I wanted to, so I picked the forty passages I thought were the most intriguing. This is the first book in the "Dear Theophilus" series. If you keep reading, I'll keep writing. My goal is to cover every book of the Bible.

The next book in this series is *Tongues of Fire: 40 Devotional Insights for Today's Church from the Book of Acts*. People on my email list will help decide what I'll cover in future books. Be sure to sign up and help pick the topic for the next book in this series.

I pray that you enjoy this book and it helps you look at your spiritual journey in a new, bold, and fresh way.

Let's get started.

Who Is Luke?

Paul is the most prolific writer in the New Testament. Who's second? That would be Dr. Luke.

Luke wrote a biography of Jesus, called "The Gospel According to Luke" (or simply "Luke"). Later he reported on the activities of the early church in "The Acts of the Apostles" (or just "Acts"). These two books account for about 25 percent of the content in the New Testament and give us valuable historical information about Jesus and his followers. Luke's writing provides a compelling two-book set that can inform our faith and enlighten the practices of our church community.

Luke was a doctor and the only non-Jewish writer in the New Testament. As such, his words are that of an outsider, which may more readily connect with those on the outside, that is, non-Jews. This includes me, and it may include you. Luke wrote with simple, yet captivating, language. He also gives us details not found in the other three biblical biographies of Jesus (Matthew, Mark, and John).

However, despite having penned two major books in the Bible—and the longest two in the New Testament—we don't know much about Luke. He's only mentioned three times in the Bible.

This is what we know:

First, we learn that Luke is a *dear friend* of Paul. Next, he's a *doctor*. Third, he's esteemed by Paul as a *fellow worker*. Last, in one of his darker hours, Paul laments that everyone is gone, and only Luke has stayed with him. As such, we see Luke as a faithful, persevering friend. Luke emerges as a man of noble character.

We also know that Luke is a firsthand observer in many of the events he records in the book of Acts. We see this through his first-person narratives in some passages when he uses the pronoun "we." (Read more about Luke and the book of Acts in this book's sequel, *Tongues of Fire: 40 Devotional Insights for Today's Church from the Book of Acts*.)

Although Luke wasn't a church leader or an apostle, his contribution to our faith and our understanding of Jesus and his church is significant. Dr. Luke's ministry function wasn't leading or preaching. Instead, he played a silent and almost unnoticed supporting role.

Though his work was quiet, his legacy lives on, loudly influencing Jesus's followers two millennia later.

What can we do to leave a faith legacy that will influence others after we die?

[Discover more in these passages about Luke in Colossians 4:14, Philemon 1:24, and 2 Timothy 4:11. Read Luke's first-person accounts in Acts 16:10–17, 20:4–15, 21:1–18, 27:1–29, 27:37, and 28:1–16.]

1.

So That You May Know

Luke 1:1–4

. . . so that you may know the certainty of the things you have been taught.

Luke 1:4

I t's easy to miss the first four verses in the book of Luke. In many Bibles, this passage carries the heading of "Introduction." Most people skip introductions. I know. I usually do.

Even if we read these first four verses, we typically read them fast. We want to get to the good stuff about John the Baptist that starts in verse five, so we can get to the really good stuff about Jesus that starts in chapter two.

We need to slow down.

Luke starts his book admitting that many others have undertaken the task of writing about the life of

Jesus. We don't know if they finished their works or what happened to their writings, but we do know Luke wants to write his own account—one thoroughly researched and backed by eyewitnesses to what Jesus said and did.

As a non-Jew, Luke carries with him the detached perspective of a religious outsider. And as a doctor he possesses the training to note details and create an accurate record. He confirms that he carefully investigated everything to write an orderly account about Jesus.

Why?

For Theophilus.

Who?

The Bible tells us nothing about Theophilus, but Luke addresses both his books to this mysterious person. The reason is significant. Luke wants Theophilus to know—for certain—the things he was taught.

Think about that.

People told Theophilus about Jesus. Perhaps Theophilus believes, but maybe he still isn't convinced. He might carry a tinge of doubt about this Jesus, the man who changed religion into a relationship. It's so countercultural that it's revolutionary. Regardless,

Luke feels it's worth his time to help Theophilus know Jesus—for sure.

If you've ever had doubts—and, if we're being honest, we all have at one time or another—wouldn't it be amazing to know for sure? Who wouldn't want to chase away lingering worries about our faith and replace them with confident conviction? That's Luke's goal. And that's precisely why we should read the book of Luke.

This is a grand undertaking that Luke made. Not only did he spend time writing a book, but even more so, he did the required research.

Luke's biography of Jesus is the longest book in the New Testament, at just under 20,000 words. His sequel, "The Book of Acts," is the second longest. Together they're almost the length of a short novel. That's a lot of words, a lot of writing, and a lot of research.

Though Luke writes this book with one person in mind, Theophilus, it's available for us two thousand years later. Like Theophilus, we too can read Luke's account of Jesus so that we can know for certain the things we've been taught.

Would we be willing to research and write a book for just one person? What other things can we do to help others be sure of their faith?

[Discover more about Theophilus in Acts 1:1–2. Read why John wrote his biography about Jesus in John 20:31.]

PART 1:

JESUS ARRIVES

Luke 1:5 to 4:13

2.

John Will Point People to Jesus

Luke 1:5–25

Both of them were righteous in the sight of God.

Luke 1:6

Zechariah and his wife Elizabeth have no kids. They're old. Seriously old. Their chance to have a baby has passed. From a human perspective it's ridiculous, yet they pray for the improbable.

They're a righteous pair, Zechariah and Elizabeth. They obey all God's commands and fully follow his rules—all of them. They're both descendants of Aaron. In addition, Zechariah's a priest. He works for God.

Did you catch all that?

They're good people. They're obedient and do the right things. They have the ideal heritage, and Zechariah lives to serve God.

For all this devotion, doesn't God owe them something in return? A kind of thank you gift? A reward? After all, they live right. In fact, Luke says they're blameless. I'm sure this is a bit of an exaggeration, a little hyperbole to make his point, but we do get the point.

Yet year after year passes and still no baby. Despite not receiving what they yearn for, they don't waver. They pray on.

Then something incredible happens.

One day the angel Gabriel shows up at Zechariah's work, right when he's supposed to burn the incense for the worship service. Talk about bad timing. The people are waiting for Zechariah to kick off their religious ceremony. Couldn't Gabriel have waited a few minutes?

But Gabriel has good news. Zechariah and Elizabeth's years of prayers are about to be answered. They'll finally have a baby, a son, in fact. And he won't be just any kid, but a special one. They're to call him John.

Gabriel says baby John will bring them much joy, and others will celebrate his birth. They must set him apart for service to God. He'll do amazing things. The Holy Spirit will empower him, and he'll spark a nationwide revival. In the mold of Elijah, he'll be super awesome. This baby boy will grow up to pave the way for the Messiah, the long-awaited Savior.

That's a lot to take in. God's people have waited for this for centuries.

And how does Zechariah respond? He says, "Really? My wife and I are too old."

Frankly, I'd say that too.

Gabriel takes this as a sign of unbelief. To make his point, he removes Zechariah's ability to talk, which makes it difficult for the poor guy to lead the people in worship. In what may be the world's first game of charades, Zechariah makes gestures to let the people know he has seen a vision from God. Astonishing.

When his stint in the temple is over, Zechariah goes home. Take time to imagine what happens when he arrives, what he communicates, and what they do. Elizabeth gets pregnant. She's overjoyed in God's blessing and his favor for taking away her shame over her childless condition. God is good.

How long are we willing to wait for God to answer our prayers and give us what we yearn for? Do we have faith to believe in the improbable? The impossible?

[Discover more in the prophesies about John the Baptist in Isaiah 40:3, Malachi 3:1, and Malachi 4:5–6 (see Matthew 11:13–14).]

Dig Deeper:

New Names for a New Thing

"See, I am doing a new thing!"

Isaiah 43:19

Did you know that there's no one in the Old Testament named John? The New Testament is the first time we read his name in the Bible. Also, did you know there's no one in the Old Testament named Jesus? The New Testament is the first time we see his name too.

It's as if God's saying, "These are new names for a new thing." Something exciting is brewing.

Do we like when God stirs up a new thing in us or is change frightening?

[Discover more about God's new thing in Isaiah 42:9, Isaiah 43:18–19, and Isaiah 48:6.]

3.

The Messiah is Coming

Luke 1:26–38

*"You will conceive and give birth to a son,
and you are to call him Jesus."*

Luke 1:31

Six months later the angel, Gabriel, makes a return visit to earth. This time it's to see Mary, a young girl, a virgin. Luke makes sure we don't miss her purity. He mentions her virgin status three times. Though engaged, she's waiting until she's married.

The exchange between Gabriel and Mary unfolds much like what happened between him and Zechariah. Gabriel's arrival startles Mary—as it would any of us. Then he tells her not to freak out—yeah, like that's possible when an angel shows up. Again, he shares news of a pregnancy, the name to give the baby, and all the remarkable things this child will grow up to do.

The virgin Mary will have a baby. This son, Jesus, is God's Son too. A descendant of Judah, he'll continue the rule of King David in a never-ending kingdom. This is what everyone's been waiting for, what the Old Testament prophets talked about for centuries.

What's Mary's response? It's almost the same as Zechariah's. Whereas he says, "How? We're old." Mary says, "How? I'm a virgin."

Gabriel saw Zechariah's understandable question as a sign of doubt and struck him mute to teach him a lesson. However, Gabriel reacts differently to Mary. He explains: "The Holy Spirit will supernaturally impregnate you." The result of this spiritual/physical union will produce a virgin birth. It's the spiritual superseding the physical—what is unseen controlling what is seen.

Then he drops some more shocking news. Elderly Elizabeth, Elizabeth-too-old-to-have-a-baby, is pregnant. If God can work a miracle in Elizabeth's aging body, he can certainly make a miracle in Mary's pure body.

Frankly, Gabriel's explanation of a supernatural conception and virgin birth doesn't help a lot. Mary, like us, knows what it takes to make a baby. Never before—and never since—has a supernatural conception like this taken place.

Personally, I'd have more questions. But not Mary. With grace and faith, she accepts Gabriel's astounding declaration as fact. She simply responds, "May it be so."

When God throws us a curveball, how do we respond? Does logic or faith guide our reaction? Can it sometimes be both?

[Discover more in these prophesies about Jesus in Psalm 145:13 and Isaiah 9:7.]

Dig Deeper:

Are We Highly Favored by God?

*The angel went to her and said, "Greetings,
you who are highly favored! The Lord
is with you."*

Luke 1:28

D o you ever wonder what God thinks of you?
I suppose that most people who consider
this question reach the wrong conclusion.
Some may think more highly of themselves than they
should, while I suspect most embrace more shame
than they ought. But what if an angel shows up and
shares God's perspective?

It's happened: An angel tells Daniel he's *highly esteemed*. This doesn't happen once, but three times,
on two occasions. Because of being highly esteemed,

God reveals profound insight about the future to Daniel.

A few centuries later, an angel tells the young girl Mary she's *highly favored*. Because of this favor, Jesus enters the world through her, and everything changes forever.

Although we can't earn our salvation, God can esteem our faith and favor our character. Implicitly, the opposite must also be true.

While we may never have an angel tell us what God thinks of us, the Bible does reveal this truth of being highly esteemed and favored. But we must read it to find out. The Holy Spirit also tells us what is true. We must listen to learn more.

Do we ever think we're highly favored by God?

[Discover more about being highly esteemed in Daniel 9:23, Daniel 10:11, and Daniel 10:19.]

4.

Mary's Road Trip

Luke 1:39–45

"As soon as the sound of your greeting reached my ears, the baby in my womb leaped for joy."

Luke 1:44

When the angel Gabriel leaves Mary, I'm sure he leaves her with thoughts of awe, astonishment, and amazement all swirling around in her young mind. Not only will her body undergo a supernatural miracle, but she is now aware that the same thing is already taking place in Elizabeth's belly.

Setting out to see Elizabeth, Mary leaves Nazareth. Alone, she heads south to the hilly part of Judea. We don't know exactly where this is, but it might have been a 30 to 50-mile trek for Mary. This would give her a lot of time to think.

Placing one foot in front of the other, the miles tick off as her journey unfolds. Aside from staying on the right road and avoiding danger, there's not much else to occupy her mind. She may wonder what will happen inside her body, how Joseph will react to her unbelievable news, and what the people of Nazareth will say about her and her supposed virgin virtue. That's a lot to ponder.

She's also likely thinking about Elizabeth. Will Mary find her pregnant, just as Gabriel said? This would give credibility to the angel's shocking message about Mary. But what if Elizabeth isn't pregnant? What would that mean? As Mary nears her destination, it's possible she struggles with a bit of doubt over Gabriel's unbelievable announcement.

I imagine Mary also prays as she walks. She may cry too. As a young teenager she has a lot to deal with.

Finally she arrives at Zechariah and Elizabeth's home. She calls out to Elizabeth. When she does, something astounding happens. The baby growing in Elizabeth's tummy leaps at the sound of Mary's voice. Though we know what it's like—either through personal experience or observation—for an unborn baby to move inside his or her mother's stomach, the idea of a baby leaping with excitement is hard to fathom. I wonder, did baby John's zeal hurt his mother?

We may recall that Gabriel told Zechariah the Holy Spirit would fill John even before he was born. John's prenatal leap gives credence to the Holy Spirit's presence in him. Then the Holy Spirit moves to also fill Elizabeth.

Though Elizabeth doesn't know about Gabriel's visit to Mary or the young girl's condition, through Holy Spirit intervention, Elizabeth boldly blesses Mary and the child she will bear. How this must comfort Mary. Not only is Elizabeth pregnant as Gabriel claimed, but she also supernaturally knows that God is at work in Mary's womb.

Then Elizabeth confirms Mary's faith, that the young girl believes God will fulfill the promises he made to her through Gabriel.

God gives his promises in the Bible. Do we believe his words in faith, like Mary, or doubt like Zechariah?

[Discover more about John the Baptist in Luke 1:13–17.]

Dig Deeper:

Two New Testament Psalms

*His father Zechariah was filled with the Holy
Spirit and prophesied.*

Luke 1:67

Mary and Zechariah both share a poem, a song of sorts. These read much like the Old Testament Psalms. The definition of a psalm is a hymn or sacred song, one often sung in celebration.

Can we call these New Testament psalms? How many other psalms are there in the Bible?

[Discover more of the Bible's songs—psalms—in Exodus 15:1–21, Judges 5, Revelation 4:8, and Revelation 5:9–10. Read what Mary said in Luke 1:46–55 and what Zechariah prophesized in Luke 1:67–79.]

Read more in the book *Beyond Psalm 150: Discover More Sacred Songs of Praise, Petition, and Lament throughout the Bible.*

5

Celebrate Jesus

Luke 2:1–20

*"I bring you good news that will cause great
joy for all the people."*

Luke 2:10

Joseph and his pregnant fiancée travel to Bethlehem for a mandatory census. Unable to find a place to stay, they hunker down in a barn. There, among the filth of livestock, Jesus is born. This is the first Christmas.

Each Christmas my attention focuses on Jesus, the real reason for our annual celebration. In considering the first Christmas, my thoughts are warm and cozy, happy and joyous, idyllic and serene. Angels sing, kings give gifts, and awed shepherds do their shepherding thing.

But all this misses that Jesus is born in someone else's barn, amid unsanitary conditions, and with the stench of animal feces filling the air. It seems so unholy, so unworthy. There's no medical team to monitor Mary's condition or aid in the birth. It's likely just Mary and Joseph trying to figure out what to do. Mary likely helped with the birth of other babies, but I wonder how much Joseph knows about the delivery process. Yet despite all this, Jesus is born.

Once the trauma of delivery passes and the messiness of birth is cleaned up, I envision an awestruck Mary gazing lovingly at this miracle that God produced in her. While nursing him, she strokes his cheek and whispers, "I love you," as only a mother can do.

As Mary overflows with joy and basks in amazement over what God has done, out in the fields a bunch of shepherds are doing their job, unaware of what has happened. Suddenly an angel shows up. He begins by saying what most angels say when they appear before humans, "Don't freak out." Even so, understandably so, the shepherds tremble at his glory. Then the angel says, "Newsflash: A baby has just been born in Bethlehem. He's the Savior. The Messiah you've been longing for." He tells them what to look for: a baby swaddled, abed in a manger.

Then, to underscore the validity of the angel's message, a grand angel choir appears. They chant their praise to God, giving him all glory and blessing the earth with the peace of his favor.

The shepherds rush to Bethlehem to check things out. Just as the angel said, they find the proud parents watching over the baby boy, Jesus, who's sleeping in the animals' feed trough. After confirming what the angel had told them, the shepherds leave and tell everyone they meet about the angel's message and Jesus's birth. Then the shepherds head back to their flocks in awe of God and what he has begun.

The shepherds believe what the angel told them, seek confirmation, and then tell everyone, praising God in the process. They're the world's first missionaries for Jesus. After they leave, Mary grows introspective, pondering and cherishing all these events in her heart.

What do we do with the good news of Jesus? Do we tell others or keep it to ourselves?

[Discover more about Jesus's birth in Matthew 2:1–23.]

6.

Two More Witnesses

Luke 2:21–38

"For my eyes have seen your salvation, which you have prepared in the sight of all nations."

Luke 2:30–31

The angels serve as the first witnesses of Jesus. They proclaim him as a Savior, the Messiah, and the Christ, which means the Anointed One. This is what the Jewish people have been waiting for. The good news about Jesus is a joyous event. But it's not just for Jews. The angel says this good news will cause immense joy for *all* people. This includes Jews *and* Gentiles. Such an idea surely shocks most Jews who assume the promised Messiah is just for them and not outsiders.

But in case we missed this first testimony about Jesus, there are two more.

A few days after Jesus's birth, his parents take him to the temple in Jerusalem to present him to God. They must go through the purification rites according to Moses's instructions, which the people have practiced for centuries. That's when they receive two more startling surprises.

First is Simeon, a godly man with Holy Spirit power. He waits in expectation of the promised Savior. God assures him he will live long enough to meet the coming Messiah. Prompted by the Holy Spirit, Simeon goes to the temple. Simeon finds baby Jesus, takes him in his arms, and praises God for what this baby will grow up to do.

What he says would surely shock any Jew familiar with the Old Testament prophecies. Simeon proclaims Jesus as the salvation sent from God—for *all* nations, not just the Jews. Jesus will light the way for Gentiles and reveal himself to them. In the process, he will be the glory of Israel. Jesus isn't here to save just the Jews, he's here to save the entire world.

Next comes Anna, an elderly woman and prophetess. She was widowed after only seven years of marriage. Anna's at least eighty-four years old when Mary and Joseph show up at the temple with Jesus.

A devout woman, she dedicates her life to God, spending as much time as possible in the temple.

She fasts, prays, and worships him. Though the Bible says she never leaves the temple and stays there night and day, consider this as an exaggeration to make the point of just how dedicated she is.

Following behind Simeon, she walks up and thanks God for Jesus, confirming he is the fulfillment of prophecy.

She recognizes him as the Savior who will redeem Jerusalem, the Messiah whom the people have expected for centuries. She thanks God and then tells everyone.

Today, it's no surprise that Jesus came to save the world, but this news would have shocked Jews 2,000 years ago. Thankfully, Jesus came to save everyone, not just a select group.

How often does God do something that challenges our expectations? When he confronts our religious assumptions, do we oppose what he's doing or embrace it in faith?

[Discover more about this religious purification ritual of babies in Exodus 13:2 and Leviticus 12:8.]

Dig Deeper:

No Need for Religious Credentials

Moved by the Spirit, he went into the temple courts.

Luke 2:27

Neither Simeon nor Anna are part of the religious elite. They lack the pedigree and the manmade credentials to do what they did. But they do have Holy Spirit wisdom. (What if Simeon had ignored God's prompting and stayed home that day?)

Holy Spirit obedience is all God needs to use them—and us—to accomplish his purposes: no special training required; no insider connections needed.

God just wants people who put him first and focus on him.

Do we let our lack of education or position keep us from doing what God calls us to do?

[Discover more about godly courage in 1 Samuel 17:45–51 and Acts 4:13. Read about Simeon in Luke 2:25–27 and Anna in Luke 2:36–37.]

7.

Tween Jesus

Luke 2:41–52

*"Didn't you know I had to be in my
Father's house?"*

Luke 2:49

After Jesus's miraculous conception, birth, and the testimonies from the angels—and later Simeon and Anna—we don't hear anything more about Jesus until he's twelve. We can only guess what his childhood might have been like. In most ways he was probably like other kids, getting into mischief and perplexing his parents. Yet in other ways, Jesus was unlike other children. He may have matured spiritually much faster than his peers. Also, Jesus didn't sin, which would make him quite unlike every other kid.

This, of course, is speculation. But here's what we do know.

Each year Mary and Joseph make a pilgrimage to Jerusalem to celebrate the Passover. When Jesus is twelve, he goes with them. This customary rite of passage shows Jesus moving from childhood into adulthood. The trip there and the Passover celebration go as expected. It's on the trip home that things go awry.

Jesus's parents and the other pilgrims head for home, moving as a group. There's safety in numbers, and camaraderie is part of the experience. Unlike today's helicopter parents who know where their kid is at every moment, Jesus's parents are much more laid-back. They assume he's with friends in another part of the caravan. It's not until the end of the first day's journey that they even look for him. But they can't find him.

In a panic, they retrace their path and rush back to Jerusalem. We don't know whether they waited until morning light or left right away. But it must have been an anxious time for them, every parent's nightmare. However, it's worse for them. *They lost the Son of God!*

After three days—three gut-wrenching, agonizing days—they finally find Jesus. He's in the temple's meeting area. He sits with the religious teachers, listening to what they say and asking questions. He responds to their questions too. His answers amaze everyone. His level of understanding impresses them. This astonishes Mary and Joseph.

Mary rebukes her son, accusing him of being irresponsible, of not caring about them and how worried they were or of their frantic search for him.

He doesn't say, "I'm sorry," or even, "I guess I lost track of time." Instead he says something shocking. He says, "Didn't you know I *had* to hang out in Papa's house?" Yes, he said he had to do this. This wasn't a preference but more so a compulsion.

Mary and Joseph don't get it. Did they forget what they heard twelve years earlier? It's more likely they remember those things said about Jesus, but they don't understand what it all meant.

Regardless, Jesus returns with them to Nazareth and obeys them. He continues to grow spiritually and physically, preparing for ministry.

Do we ever feel that we've lost Jesus? What do we do to find him? How do we react when we do?

[Discover more about lost things in Luke 15.]

8

The Real Message of John the Baptist

Luke 3:1–14

"Anyone who has two shirts should share with the one who has none, and anyone who has food should do the same."

Luke 3:11

Our timeline jumps forward eighteen years, and we pick up the story with John the Baptist—John for short. This is the second time we hear about him. And there will be one more time that Luke weaves him into Jesus's story.

We begin with a curious phrase that's easy to overlook. Luke writes that *word came from God to John.* This is another case of the Holy Spirit providing God-given instruction to his people. Though we don't know what this instruction is, we do know that John acts. He goes on a tour in the area, a circuit preacher of sorts. His message is simple. He baptizes people who are sorry for the wrong things they've done and want to turn their life around. The Bible uses the words *sin* and *repentance* to describe this.

John's message spreads, and throngs flock to him so he can baptize them. However, instead of embracing this and seeing it as affirmation of his work, he challenges the people. "You're a brood of snakes." That's no way to grow a ministry or amass a following.

But baptism isn't enough. John wants to see changed lives too.

The people ask him to explain what they should do.

John starts by giving a general instruction for them to produce fruit—that is, do good things—to confirm they've changed. Then he gives two specific examples. He says anyone with two shirts (or two of anything, I suppose) should give one to someone who's shirtless. Even more convicting, he says anyone with food should share with someone who's hungry.

Next he gives some specific examples of two occupations, jobs that don't command the respect of the Jewish people. One group is tax collectors—who historically exploited the people. The other group is soldiers—who often abused their power.

To the tax collectors John says, "Don't collect more than what you're supposed to." And to the soldiers, presumably Roman soldiers, John gives three instructions. First, "Don't extort money." Next, "Don't falsely accuse anyone." Last, "Be content with your pay."

This is quite a list. Let's put these items into today's context:

- Give our extra possessions to those in need.
- Share food with the hungry.
- Be fair and honest in financial dealings.
- Don't use our position to wrongly increase our wealth.
- Don't accuse people without proof.
- Don't complain about our paychecks.

Though we think of John's message as baptism, we miss the point. His real message is changing our behavior.

Baptism isn't the end; it's the beginning. What should we do to show others our baptism was real?

[Discover more about putting our faith into action in James 2:14–26. Read more about John the Baptist in Isaiah 40:3–5 and Luke 7:18–35.]

9

The Mystery of Jesus's Baptism

Luke 3:15–22

"You are my Son, whom I love; with you I am well pleased."

Luke 3:22

When the people ask John if he's the Messiah, whom the Old Testament prophets foretold, he tells them he's not, but he's indirect about it.

By way of an answer, John explains that he baptizes with water (to signify remorse for our mistakes), but someone much greater will soon come. This Messiah is more powerful than John. John says he's unworthy to even bend down to tie the Savior's shoelaces. Instead of water, this Messiah will baptize people with the Holy Spirit and fire. Whatever this means, it sounds extraordinary.

Though some attempt to connect New Testament baptism with Old Testament uses of water in religious ceremonies and rituals, any correlation seems weak.

Definitions of baptism use the words *cleanse* and *purify*, among others. This helps some, since the first few books of the Old Testament talk a lot about cleansing and purification. Yet pulling the ceremony of baptism from this seems a stretch.

The word *baptize* only occurs in the New Testament. Prior to John performing his water ceremony, it's never mentioned. The Old Testament doesn't talk about baptism, and there's no biblical account of its origin. It seems to have just started on its own, beginning with John. Did he invent it? Perhaps God told him to do this new thing, pointing people to a new way—Jesus.

Further confusing the issue, in a curious passage in Corinthians, Paul talks about the Old Testament Israelites in the desert undergoing some sort of baptism *into* Moses. Yet the Old Testament doesn't record this event. So we can assume this was a figurative baptism, not an actual one.

None of this, however, gets us any closer to understanding the basis behind baptism. But what's important is that Jesus later tells us to do it.

John, by the way, baptizes Jesus.

Why?

Jesus's baptism is mysterious—because he's sinless and doesn't need to repent of anything. It's also awe-inspiring—because Papa shows up.

As part of his baptism, Jesus prays. When he prays, heaven opens, allowing a glimpse into the spiritual realm. The people see the Holy Spirit come down. He visually descends in a form that resembles a dove. Then, to underscore this extraordinary event, a voice booms from heaven. It's Father God. He speaks to Jesus. He says, "You're my boy. I so love you. I'm most pleased with you and what you're doing."

Jesus, the Son of God, comes to earth and pleases his Father in heaven. And this is just the beginning.

Why did Jesus, who didn't sin, feel John should baptize him?

[Discover more about baptism in Matthew 28:19, Acts 2:1–4, and 1 Corinthians 10:1–2.]

10.

Strike Three

Luke 4:1–13

*When the devil had finished all this tempting,
he left him until an opportune time.*

Luke 4:13

With his baptism behind him and the Holy Spirit in him, Jesus leaves John the Baptist at the Jordan River. Instead of launching into his earthly ministry—seemingly the perfect time to do so—Jesus obeys the Holy Spirit who sends him into the wilderness.

What?

There aren't any people there. How can Jesus save the world if he's not with the people who need saving? Though this is counterintuitive, it's part of God's plan to prepare Jesus for ministry.

While in the desert, Jesus fasts. We don't know if this is because the Holy Spirit told him to or because there's no food in the desert. Regardless, he goes without eating for a long time, for forty days. That's over five weeks with no food. Then Luke adds a detail we readily understand: Jesus is hungry.

The devil, who wants to thwart Jesus's mission, jumps on this opportunity to derail a physically weak Jesus before he can start his work. The devil (Luke doesn't call him Satan) tempts Jesus into using his godly power in ways he shouldn't and to cut his journey short.

First, aware of how hungry Jesus is, the devil taunts him. Mocking him, the devil says, "If you're really God, just make this stone turn into a loaf of bread." What a clever idea. In an instant Jesus could have all the nourishment his food-deprived body craves. Why hadn't he thought of this sooner?

But Jesus doesn't give in to this easy solution. He quotes from the Law of Moses, "Bread isn't enough. We need God's word to truly live."

That's strike one against the devil.

Next, in an instant, the devil shows Jesus all the kingdoms and people in the world. The devil, who presently has authority over it all, promises to give everything to Jesus. But there's one catch. Jesus must worship him. Though the payoff would be huge, the cost would be even greater.

Jesus again quotes from the Law. He reminds the devil, "Fear God and only serve him."

Strike two.

In his third attempt, the devil throws some Scripture at Jesus, quoting from the book of Psalms. Here's the setup: The devil baits Jesus, taunting him to take a high dive off the temple's pinnacle. He reminds Jesus that God has angels watching us. "They'll lift us up when we fall, so that we won't even stub our toe." By jumping, Jesus could show God's power. And if the angels don't rescue Jesus and he dies when he falls, that would serve the devil's purpose.

Jesus's comeback is succinct: "Don't test God."

Strike three.

Having struck out, the devil leaves to make a new plan to take Jesus down.

When we face temptation, do we attempt to resist it on our own or cite Scripture to put the devil in his place?

[Discover more in the Scripture Jesus quotes in Deuteronomy 6:13 & 16 and Deuteronomy 8:3. Read the passage Satan quotes in Psalm 91:11–12.]

PART 2:

JESUS SERVES

Luke 4:14 to 19:27

11.

People Try to Kill Jesus

Luke 4:14–30

*The people in the synagogue were furious
when they heard this.*

Luke 4:28

After the devil strikes out in his attempt to stop Jesus before he can even start his ministry, the Holy Spirit sends Jesus to Galilee. There he instructs the people in the synagogues, and they praise him. Then Jesus goes to Nazareth, his hometown, for the Sabbath.

He reads from the book of Isaiah to the people gathered there. The passage contains a future-focused prophecy about the coming Messiah. Here are the key points Jesus reads: God's spirit is in me, and he's anointed me to:

- tell the poor about God's good news,

- let the prisoners know about freedom,

- heal blind people,

- free the oppressed, and

- proclaim God's favor.

Then Jesus sits. Everyone watches him. Next he says, "Yep, that text is about me and what I'm going to do." They're amazed at his words and speak highly of him.

If only Jesus had stopped. Instead he launches into a teaching.

These people know him. He grew up here. They're his tribe. He's blunt. "People never accept a hometown prophet." Then he reminds them of two stories.

First, he mentions the prophet Elijah, who during a three-year drought leaves the country of Israel and travels to Zarephath, in Sidon. There he meets a poor widow, preparing a final meal for her and her son before they die of starvation.

Miraculously, God multiplies her meager supply of flour and oil to feed her, her son, and Elijah throughout the drought. Though there are many needy widows in Israel, God sent Elijah to help a foreigner.

Next, Jesus mentions Naaman, the commander of the Syrian army that has oppressed the nation of Israel. Naaman has leprosy, and the prophet Elisha heals him, even though many people in the nation of Israel also have leprosy. Not only does God direct Elisha to heal a foreigner, but this foreigner has oppressed God's people.

These examples show God favoring those outside his chosen people—and doing so at their expense.

The people rage against Jesus for mentioning these two stories. Though everything he said is true, the people don't care. His teaching insults them. A mob forms, they drive him out of town, and try to throw him off a cliff to kill him. But it's not his time. Jesus just walks through the crowd and leaves, unscathed.

When we hear a message that offends us, do we attack the messenger even though it's true?

[Discover more about Isaiah's prophesy in Isaiah 61:1–2. Read the stories Jesus refers to in 1 Kings 17:7–16 and 2 Kings 5:1–14.]

12.

Jesus's First Miracles

Luke 4:31–44

And the news about him spread throughout the surrounding area.

Luke 4:37

After Jesus leaves Nazareth unharmed, he heads to Capernaum, another town in Galilee. At this point in Luke's account, Jesus hasn't performed any miracles. That's about to change.

In the synagogue Jesus encounters a demon-possessed man. The guy has an evil or impure spirit in him. When the demon/man sees Jesus, he yells, "Hey, I know you! You're Jesus, God's holy one. Have you come to destroy us?"

Jesus doesn't answer. Instead he bellows, "Silence!" Then he commands the demon to leave the man. The demon does, and the man is unharmed.

Jesus's authority and power to control a demon shocks the people. The news of this miracle spreads quickly.

Next Jesus goes to Simon's home (who Matthew identifies as Peter, as in Simon Peter, one of the twelve disciples). His mother-in-law is sick with a high fever. Her family asks Jesus to help. He commands the fever to leave her body, and it does. Then she gets up and makes them a meal.

By the end of the day, people flock to Jesus with their various illnesses and demon possessions. He lays his hands on the sick and heals each one. As for the demons, he casts them out. Some shout, "You're the Son of God!" But Jesus doesn't appreciate their testimony and commands them to be quiet.

It takes Jesus all night to heal the sick and release the possessed. By daybreak Jesus heads out for some alone time to rest and pray, but the people seek him out and beg him to stay. However, he moves on. He must preach the good news of God's kingdom in other towns.

Though he could have stayed and built a ministry in Capernaum, this isn't what he came to earth to do. He continues his mission, leaving the people in Capernaum in awe over his supernatural power to heal and cast out demons.

The people beg Jesus to stay because of what he can do for them. Is that enough of a reason for us to seek Jesus?

[Discover more about Peter's mother-in-law in Matthew 8:14–17 and Mark 1:30–31.]

Dig Deeper:

Evil Spirits and Demon Possession

At that very time Jesus cured many who had diseases, sicknesses and evil spirits, and gave sight to many who were blind.

Luke 7:21

In the Bible we run across the phrase "*evil spirit.*" (Alternate phrases are "*impure spirit,*" "*unclean spirit,*" and "*corrupting spirit.*") *Evil spirit* occurs twelve times in the Bible, six in Luke's writing. *Demon-possessed* occurs twenty-one times in the Bible, five in Luke's writing.

What is an evil spirit anyway? Is it the same as being demon-possessed? Probably so.

Consider these four ideas about understanding evil spirits and demon possession.

- As a teenager, I thought an evil spirit and demon possession were merely ancient man's way of understanding mental illness.

- As a young adult, my perspective flipped. I thought mental illness was merely modern man's logical attempt to explain evil spirits and demon possession.

- Later I began to consider that both mental illness and evil spirits/demon possession existed but as different phenomena.

- Now I wonder if these are just two ways of looking at the same thing—one from a spiritual perspective and the other from a physical perspective.

Although debating the meaning of evil spirits and demon possession may be stimulating to discuss, the main point is that Jesus makes these people's lives better—and he gives his followers the authority to do the same.

How should we understand evil spirits and demon possession today?

[Discover more about evil spirits in 1 Samuel 16:14–23, 1 Samuel 18:10, 1 Samuel 19:9, Luke 8:2, and Acts 19:11–16. Read more about demon possession in Luke 8:26–38, Luke 9:37–42, and Acts 19:13.]

13.

Fishing for People

Luke 5:1–11

"Don't be afraid, from now on you will fish for people."

Luke 5:10

At this time in our story, Jesus and Simon (as in Simon Peter or just Peter) have already met. Remember, Jesus went to Simon's home, healed his mother-in-law, and stayed for dinner. However, Jesus hasn't yet picked his main twelve disciples.

The next time we see Jesus and Simon together, Jesus stands at the edge of a lake, instructing the people. Anxious to hear better and be closer to him, they crowd in. This threatens to push Jesus into the water. There are a couple of boats nearby and Jesus climbs into one of them. He asks the owner, Simon, to push out into the lake.

Sound carries well across water, so with Jesus speaking from a boat, the people can hear him better. When Jesus finishes teaching, he turns to Simon and says, "Push out further. Drop your nets, and let's catch some fish." Though Simon may assume Jesus is hungry and wants fish for lunch, Jesus has something else in mind.

Simon tells Jesus that they fished all night and didn't catch a thing.

Now, Simon knows how to fish. This is his trade, his livelihood. When it comes to fishing, he's an expert. Jesus, however, isn't a fisherman. He's a carpenter. He knows how to make things with his hands. He's an expert at woodworking.

So when the professional fisherman hasn't caught a thing, it seems strange for the experienced carpenter to offer fishing tips. But that's exactly what Jesus does to Simon. The novice tells the expert what to do.

Logically, it would have been reasonable for Simon to ignore Jesus's rookie advice. After all, Simon has been fishing his entire life. Jesus hasn't.

Yet Simon sets aside his pride and disregards his experience. He agrees to do what Jesus asked, "just because you say so."

The results astound Simon. His nets fill with fish; they're about to break. He calls his partners in the other boat to help. Soon both boats are full of fish, so full that they could sink. This huge catch astonishes the fishermen.

It also defies logic and all that Simon knows is true. The only explanation is that he's seen a miracle. He falls before Jesus and says, "I'm a sinful man. I don't deserve to be in your presence.

Jesus doesn't leave, however. Instead he says, "Don't be afraid." Jesus prepares to change Simon's life forever. "From now on you will fish for people."

Simon and his fishing partners bring their boats to shore and leave everything behind to follow Jesus.

Sometimes what God tells us to do seems foolish. We may think we know better and ignore him. But we should do it anyway, just because he says so.

[Discover more about the disciples fishing in Luke 5:4–11 and John 21:3–14.]

14.

To Forgive and to Heal

Luke 5:17–26

"Which is easier: to say, 'Your sins are forgiven,' or to say, 'Get up and walk'"?

Luke 5:23

J esus specializes in doing the unexpected. This story is no exception.

It seems Jesus will teach people anyplace he can, anywhere people gather. This time he's teaching in a home. There are lots of religious people there. Though we don't know their motives—whether to hear Jesus or to criticize him—the important thing is that they are there.

Knowing of Jesus's reputation to heal people, some guys carry their paralyzed friend to him. They try to take him into the house, but they can't because there are too many people. Desperate, they climb up onto the roof, open some tiles, and lower their paralyzed friend into the room, right in front of Jesus.

The visual image seems incredible.

First, I don't know the construction of homes 2,000 years ago, but could they do this without damaging the house? At the very least they disrupt Jesus's teaching as they work to lower their friend. And I often wonder why they didn't try a little harder to push their way through the crowd or simply wait for Jesus to leave the house after he finished teaching. Apparently, they see a rooftop entry as their best option.

The man's problem is obvious. He can't walk. Everyone can see that. But Jesus doesn't heal this man—at least not at first. Instead, he does the unexpected. He says, "Your sins are forgiven."

Jesus realizes this man's *greatest* need isn't physical but spiritual. So it is with God. Sometimes we don't get what we expect, but we always get what we need.

The religious teachers are aghast at Jesus. They charge him with blasphemy. *Only God can forgive sins*, they think.

Jesus knows their thoughts and asks them a challenging question. "What's easier, to forgive someone's sins or to heal them?"

Knowing that it's easier to say, "Your sins are forgiven" than to make a lame man walk, Jesus heals the man too. This addresses the man's second greatest need. In doing this, Jesus proves he has the power to forgive sins, as well.

Jesus shows that he came not only to save us (forgive our sins), but he also came to heal us. Jesus often does or says the unexpected. Perhaps that's one reason why the crowds flocked to him two thousand years ago and why we're drawn to him today.

Unexpected Jesus may surprise us, and at times perplex us, but he's still our Savior and our healer. All we need to do is accept him for his saving power *and* his healing power.

What do we expect from Jesus: forgiveness, healing, or both?

[Discover more about this account in Matthew 9:2–8 and Mark 2:2–12.]

15.

What's the Deal with Sunday?

Luke 6:1–11

*"I ask you, which is lawful on the Sabbath:
to do good or to do evil, to save life or to
destroy it?*

Luke 6:9

Most Christians uphold Sunday as their special day to focus on God, a day of rest. They go to church to worship and serve him. They may also do special activities and avoid doing other things, all because it's Sunday.

The Bible never tells us to set Sunday aside. Instead, it focuses on the Sabbath, the *last* day of the week from a Jewish perspective. Traditionally that would be Saturday. The Old Testament gives a lot of instructions about what the people can and cannot do on the Sabbath. For the people of Jesus's day, these instructions had expanded into a voluminous collection of specific, manmade details covering what's allowed and what's not. The people, especially religious ones, pursue these rules with a legalistic zeal.

Again, doing the unexpected, Jesus confronts the people and their religious practices.

One Sabbath, Jesus and his disciples walk through a field. This likely pushes religious boundaries, as Sabbath travel is limited. Then Jesus allows his disciples to pick some grain, rub off the husk, and eat the seeds. Though the Old Testament Law doesn't prohibit eating on the Sabbath, it does prohibit work. The disciples, in their small act of feeding themselves, harvest grain and prepare food on the Sabbath.

That is a no-no for the religious zealots. They criticize Jesus for his disciples' unlawful action on the Sabbath.

He reminds them of King David, running for his life. He goes to a priest and asks for food. The only thing available is the special bread, reserved for the priests. The priest gives it to David even though the Law prohibits it.

On another Sabbath, Jesus goes to the synagogue and teaches the people. A man with a deformed hand is there. The religious leaders watch to see what Jesus will do. They're looking for a reason to criticize him. Jesus knows what they're thinking.

He calls the man with the deformed hand to stand before them. Then he asks, "Should we do good things on the Sabbath or evil?" That gets their attention. Then he tells the man to stretch out his hand. As the man does, his hand is fully restored.

Though the religious teachers should be happy for this man, who regained the full use of his hand, instead they're furious at Jesus for "working" on the Sabbath. Instead of praising God's healing power, they criticize God's Son.

What does the Sabbath mean to us? Are we open to skip church to help someone?

[Discover more about Sabbath behavior in Matthew 12:1–14, Mark 2:23–28, Luke 13:10–16, and Luke 14:1–6. Read about King David's plight in 1 Samuel 21:1–6.]

Dig Deeper:

The Twelve Disciples

*When morning came, he called his disciples
to him and chose twelve of them, whom he
also designated apostles.*

Luke 6:13

We know that Jesus had twelve disciples, right? This number occurs repeatedly in all four gospels. And the first three list them by name. Unfortunately, the lists don't completely match.

Matthew and Mark list Simon Peter, Andrew, James (son of Zebedee), John, Philip, Bartholomew, Thomas, Matthew, James (son of Alphaeus), Thaddaeus, Simon the Zealot, and Judas Iscariot.

Luke matches eleven of these names, but he includes Judas (the son of James) and omits Thaddaeus.

John doesn't provide a list but does mention some disciples by name: Andrew, Simon Peter, Philip,

Judas Iscariot, and Thomas. Indirectly included are John and James ("the sons of Zebedee"). However, John implies Nathanael is a disciple too. Jesus tells Nathanael, "follow me" and he does, but he's not even mentioned in the other three gospels.

So that ups the count of disciples to fourteen. How can this be? Here are some possible explanations:

They Use Nicknames: If we assume that Thaddaeus was also known as Judas (the son of James), as well as Nathanael, that explains everything, but this is quite a stretch.

Some Lists Are Wrong: Matthew and Mark completely agree, so their lists must be right while Luke and John must have each made a mistake.

The Group Was Dynamic: Though Jesus only had twelve disciples, there was an ebb and flow over his three years of ministry as disciples came and went.

Twelve Is Not an Absolute Number: We live in a culture that assumes precision. If we say twelve, we mean twelve. No more and no less. We don't mean *about* twelve or twelve, give or take a couple; we mean twelve.

While Jesus's disciples might have changed over time, it's more likely that the label of "The Twelve" was an approximate number for the sake of convenience.

Jesus's ~~twelve~~ fourteen disciples are:

- Andrew
- Bartholomew
- James (son of Alphaeus)
- James (son of Zebedee)
- John
- Judas Iscariot
- Judas (son of James)
- Matthew
- Nathanael
- Philip
- Simon Peter
- Simon the Zealot
- Thaddaeus
- Thomas

Are we concerned that Jesus may not have actually had twelve disciples?

[Discover more about the names of Jesus's disciples in Matthew 10:2–4, Mark 3:16–19, Luke 6:13–16, John 1:43–51, and John 21:1–2.]

16.

The Sermon on the Plain

Luke 6:17–49

*He went down with them and stood on
a level place.*

Luke 6:17

You may have heard of Jesus's best-known sermon, the Sermon on the Mount, which Matthew records in his biography of Jesus. The sermon gets its name because it happens on the side of a mountain—a mount, if you will. That's why we call it the Sermon on the Mount.

Luke also records a lengthy sermon, but this one doesn't occur on the side of a mountain. Instead it happens on a level place, a plain or possibly a plateau. To distinguish this sermon from the one Matthew records, let's call this one the Sermon on the Plain.

Before Jesus delivers his Sermon on the Plain, something significant happens. The people flock to Jesus, not only to hear him, but also for him to heal them from their diseases and cure them from their evil spirits. And here's the interesting part, Luke says *all* the people try to touch him, because power flows from him, the power to heal.

After Jesus meets the physical needs of the people, he's ready to teach them—and they're ready to listen.

Jesus begins with a series of encouragements to those who struggle. He starts each one saying, "Blessed are you . . . ," which he follows up with a promise of provision.

He moves to a series of warnings to people who seem to have it good. He starts each one of these saying, "Woe to you . . . ," which he follows up with a somber look into their future. Through these two series, Jesus lifts the downtrodden and warns the prosperous.

Next, he talks about loving our enemies and showing mercy, just as God shows us mercy. Then Jesus warns against judging others and the importance of forgiving. To the degree we forgive, we will receive forgiveness.

Don't rush past this.

To receive full forgiveness from God, we must forgive others fully. To be forgiven, we must forgive first.

Then he slips in a parable about the foolishness of a blind person trying to lead another blind person. A second parable considers the hypocrisy of trying to help someone overcome a minor problem when the first person's dilemma is greater.

Jesus moves from this into another example. We can identify a tree by the fruit that grows on its branches. So too, good people do good things, but evil comes from those with evil hearts.

To wrap up his Sermon on the Plain, Jesus contrasts wise builders with foolish ones. The wise ones build a solid foundation, which is what we do when we put Jesus's words into practice.

The Sermon on the Mount and the Sermon on the Plain have similar passages, but they're different events. Because Jesus speaks to many groups, in many places, it's logical that he tailors each message to his audience, giving them precisely what they need to hear.

Jesus also gives us what we need to hear when we need it. All we need to do is listen to what he says—and then obey.

When God speaks to us, do we listen?

[Discover more in the Sermon on the Mount in Matthew 5–7.]

17.

Faith or Grace?

Luke 7:1–17

"Lord, don't trouble yourself, for I do not deserve to have you come under my roof."

Luke 7:6

A military leader, a centurion, wants Jesus to heal his dying servant, a valued attendant. However, the centurion doesn't approach Jesus himself. Instead he calls in a favor. He asks some Jewish leaders to go on his behalf. If these men are like most of the religious leaders we read about in the Bible, they don't like Jesus. It must humiliate them to ask him for help.

In presenting their case, the Jewish leaders claim the centurion is worthy to receive Jesus's aid. This perspective matches the Jewish understanding of the Old Testament, which they see as focusing on right behavior.

Despite the admirable qualities of the centurion, the reality is that no one is worthy, no one deserves God's favor. But though we can't earn God's attention, he gives it anyway.

Jesus agrees to help, but the centurion deems himself unworthy to meet Jesus or for Jesus to even enter his home. Again, speaking through others, the centurion gives us a lesson in authority. Just as he has authority over his troops, he acknowledges that Jesus has authority over his servant's illness. "Just say the word," he says, "and it will happen." The centurion's faith—greater than any Jesus has seen from his own people—amazes the Savior. He heals the servant in that instant.

Later Jesus travels with his disciples to the city of Nain. A huge crowd follows. As he approaches the city gate, he meets a funeral procession. It's for the only son of a widow. In that culture, a widow with no sons has no means of support. (This isn't God's plan. It's man's perversion of it.) Her future holds only poverty and despair.

Jesus sees her situation. He feels her pain—not only her agony over losing her only son, but also her worry of a bleak future. Though she asks Jesus for nothing, he's moved to help. He tells her not to cry, touches the coffin, and says to the dead man, "Young man, get up!"

The guy sits up and begins talking. (Imagine that happening at a funeral we're at.) Jesus gives the widow's resurrected son back to her.

Awe fills everyone. They praise God. They esteem Jesus as an amazing prophet, one sent from God to help them. The news of what Jesus did spreads throughout the area.

For the centurion, Jesus heals the man's servant because of the centurion's faith in Jesus's power. The centurion receives a miracle because he asks for it in faith.

For the widow, Jesus raises her son from the dead, not because she asks him to, but because he has compassion for her. The widow receives a miracle because Jesus offers her grace.

Sometimes we need faith, and sometimes grace is enough.

Do we ever strive to be worthy of God's attention when his grace is all we need?

[Discover more about God's grace for us in 2 Corinthians 12:9.]

18.

Jesus Assures John the Baptist

Luke 7:18–35

*"Go back and report to John what you have
seen and heard."*

Luke 7:22

John the Baptist appears three times in Luke's biography of Jesus. First, Luke writes about John's birth and the events that lead up to it. Next, Luke records John's baptism of Jesus. Now, we read about John one final time.

John languishes in prison, landing there unjustly after criticizing Herod for marrying his brother's wife.

With time to think, I imagine John wonders why Jesus doesn't come to visit him. Couldn't Jesus, the Son of God, free him from prison? Isn't he supposed to set the captives free? That's what he said he came to do.

John merely did what God called him to do. Why should he suffer for it? Maybe these thoughts flood John's mind as he sits in prison, or maybe not.

Regardless, John sends two of his disciples to ask Jesus a question, a critical one. "Are you the person the prophets wrote about, or should we wait for someone else?" This question suggests a tinge of doubt in John's mind about who Jesus is. I suspect John seeks confirmation that his work wasn't in vain. He wants to know his life mattered.

John's disciples track down Jesus and ask him this question. They approach Jesus as he heals people from their diseases, illnesses, and evil spirits. He even restores sight to the blind.

Jesus doesn't directly answer their question. Instead he tells them to report to John what they've seen and heard. He instructs them to tell John that the blind can now see, the lame now walk, the lepers now have clear skin, the deaf now hear, and the dead now live. In addition, the poor are hearing the good news. To wrap up his message for John, Jesus concludes with what could appear as a rebuke, "fortunate are those who don't trip because of me," but it's actually encouragement for John to stay strong and not doubt.

John's disciples leave. Then Jesus launches into a teaching about John's life and ministry. Jesus makes three key points.

First, he confirms John is the person the Old Testament prophets predicted would pave the way for the Messiah.

Next, Jesus affirms there's no person on earth more important than John, but in the kingdom of God we will *all* be greater than John.

Third, Jesus gives us a lesson about people with a religious spirit. When John followed his restricted diet, as God commanded, the people criticized him. Then when Jesus came he ate and drank freely, and the people criticized him for that.

So too for us. Whatever we do, it seems someone will complain.

How do we react when we're wrongly criticized? Have we ever criticized things we didn't understand? What about things we didn't like?

[Discover more about Jesus coming to set captives free in Isaiah 61:1 and Luke 4:18. Read about Herod and John the Baptist in Luke 3:19–20 and Luke 9:7–9. Learn about others wrongly imprisoned and then freed in Acts 5:18–20 and Acts 12:5–11.]

Dig Deeper:

The Women Who Anoint Jesus

As she stood behind him at his feet weeping,
she began to wet his feet with her tears.

Luke 7:38

Each of the four accounts of Jesus's life—Matthew, Mark, Luke, and John—give a story about a woman who anoints Jesus with expensive perfume, but the details in each report vary. It may be that this happens on four separate occasions. Or it could be the same story, with a few details that differ. Or perhaps it's somewhere in between.

Matthew and Mark's accounts are the closest, with the only difference being who criticizes her for wasting expensive perfume: Matthew says it's the disciples. Mark says it's some people. Matthew and Mark likely cover the same event.

In John's version, the woman who anoints Jesus is Mary, sister of Martha and Lazarus, but in the other three reports, we don't know the woman's name. John's version is like Matthew and Mark's, but one key difference is that this woman anoints Jesus's feet, not his head as in the first two accounts. Also, John names just one person who criticizes her: Judas Iscariot. Last, John says that Martha is serving dinner in Jesus's honor, so we assume it's at her home, whereas Matthew and Mark say Jesus is hanging out at Simon the leper's house.

Luke's version differs the most. First, he calls her a sinful woman, something not even hinted at in the other accounts. Next, his version takes place at a Pharisee's home. His name is Simon, but it doesn't say he's a leper. And there's no mention of it being in Bethany, as with the other three versions.

In Luke's story, a woman comes up behind Jesus as he reclines at the dinner table. She weeps at his feet, apparently in sorrow for her wayward actions. Her tears fall on him and she uses her hair to dry his feet. Then she dumps her perfume on his feet.

In this account, the woman doesn't receive criticism, but Jesus does. The Pharisee thinks that Jesus should have known the woman touching him is a sinner. Jesus affirms the woman for washing his feet, something his host didn't do. Then he forgives her for her many sins, confirms her saving faith, and sends her off in peace. Luke's account contains enough differences that it's likely a separate event.

It doesn't really matter if this event happened once, twice, three times, or even four, where it happened, or who was involved. What counts is the lavish adoration given to Jesus. May this passage inspire us to do the same.

What can we do to show our adoration of Jesus?

[Discover more about these stories in Matthew 26:6–13, Mark 14:3–9, Luke 7:36–50, and John 12:1–8.]

19.

Anointing Jesus

Luke 7:36–50

"Your faith has saved you; go in peace."

Luke 7:50

Our next story opens with an interesting line. It says a Pharisee, named Simon, invites Jesus over for dinner.

Don't rush past this.

Pharisees are religious insiders. They follow the Law of Moses with much zeal. In addition, they adhere to thousands of other rules they made up over the years to guide them in rightly following the Law of Moses. To their credit, they are righteous, but they're also legalistic—to the max. Today's most legalistic person wouldn't come close to matching their rigid, controlled existence.

Though Jesus loves everyone—including Pharisees, religious leaders, and insider Jews—he does criticize them. This is because they miss the point of what God intended when he gave his instructions to Moses. Jesus wants to change their perspective. In response, they oppose him. So it seems strange that a Pharisee would seek out Jesus, let alone want to eat with him. But that's exactly what the Pharisee, Simon, does. However, when Jesus shows up, Simon doesn't offer him the socially appropriate welcome for their culture: wash his feet, greet him with a kiss, or anoint his head.

Jesus, Simon, and the rest of his guests recline at Simon's table. Now, if you envision Leonardo da Vinci's painting, The Last Supper, with people sitting at a table, you have the wrong image. At Simon's home, they lay on their side, leaning on their elbow, with their heads toward a low table and their legs pointing away. Hold that image.

A woman with a sinful lifestyle approaches Jesus. Surely Simon hadn't invited her, so she must have crashed the party. She arrives ready to show Jesus how much she loves him. This might be her only chance. She stands behind his feet (recall the image of him reclining at the table). Emotion overcomes her. She weeps profusely. Her tears fall on Jesus's feet. Lacking a towel to dry them, she uses the only resource available:

her hair. She kisses his feet too. Then she pours her perfume over Jesus's feet. She doesn't dab it on; she empties the bottle. Lavishly. The aroma fills the room.

In his mind, Simon judges them as only a Pharisee can. Mentally he criticizes the woman for her inappropriate lifestyle and Jesus for allowing a sinful woman to touch him, since he should know what kind of woman she was.

Jesus, knowing Simon's thoughts, gives a quick parable about forgiveness. Then Jesus recounts how Simon neglected to wash and dry Jesus's feet, greet him with a kiss, and put oil on him when he arrived. But this woman did all those things.

Jesus says to her, "Your sins are forgiven." As the other guests murmur, Jesus adds, "Because of your faith, you are saved."

The woman's path to salvation is simple: worship Jesus and love him.

Is worshiping Jesus and loving him enough for us to be saved?

[Discover more about saving faith in Romans 10:10, Ephesians 2:8, and Hebrews 10:39.]

Dig Deeper:

Jesus Eats with Pharisees

"One of the Pharisees invited Jesus to have dinner with him."

Luke 7:36

Did you notice where Jesus is when the woman anoints him? I said to not to rush past that. He's at the home of a Pharisee. Though it's not surprising that Jesus is at a Pharisee's home, it is surprising that a Pharisee invites Jesus over for a meal.

This is because Jesus often criticizes Pharisees for their legalistic approach to life, for turning a relationship with God into a religion that oppresses people and serves to keep them from God. For a Pharisee to extend a dinner invitation to Jesus would be opening himself up to criticism. Who'd want that?

What's even more surprising is that this doesn't happen once, but three times in the book of Luke.

Since we won't cover the other two, here are all three times a Pharisee invites Jesus over for a meal:

- Luke 7:36–50
- Luke 11:37–54
- Luke 14:1–14

Each time Jesus uses the occasion to teach truth to his dinner companions. And, either directly or indirectly, he criticizes his host. That's no way to get invited back, but for Jesus, being who he is, I doubt he cares.

How would we react if someone criticized our beliefs or practices in front of our guests?

[Discover more about another Pharisee interacting with Jesus in John 3:1–21.]

20

The Parable of the Sower

Luke 8:4–15

*"The seed on good soil stands for those with
a noble and good heart, who hear the word,
retain it, and by persevering produce a crop."*

Luke 8:15

Luke records many of Jesus's parables. What makes this one unique is that Luke also shares Jesus's explanation of it. This is important to make sure that his disciples—and we—don't get it wrong.

Two thousand years ago people probably planted seeds manually, cupping the seeds in their hand and then scattering them across the ground. Though this gave them control over where the seeds went, they didn't have complete control. Some seeds ended up in places where they wouldn't thrive. This is the point of Jesus's parable.

Let's pick up the story. A large crowd gathers. Jesus seizes the opportunity to teach them:

A farmer sows seeds in his field. As he scatters the seeds, some fall on the walking path. They'll never amount to anything. Not only will people step on them, but birds will swoop down and eat them.

Other seeds fall on rocks. Though they may germinate, without dirt for them to send roots into, they'll soon die. (Side note: We must make sure our faith is well rooted. Those roots are in the Bible.)

Another group of seeds fall among a bunch of weeds. Though the seeds will sprout, the weeds will choke them out, and they'll soon die.

However, most seeds fall on good soil. These seeds shoot up and produce a nice yield—a hundred-fold. Then Jesus tacks on this concluding thought. He says, "If you have ears, then you better listen."

To us, the meaning of this parable is clear. However, this isn't the case with his disciples. They ask him to explain:

As with every parable, the elements of the story represent something. The seed is the spoken word of

God. The crowd hears the word of God, but they react differently.

Those represented by the path hear what God says, but the devil swoops in and snatches it from their hearts. This keeps them from believing and being saved.

The rocky area represents people who hear the word of God with much joy, but their faith doesn't produce roots. Having nothing to keep them in place, after a while they forget God's message and move on to other things.

The seed that falls among the weeds represents still others who hear the word of God, but the worries of life choke out their faith, and they never mature.

The seed that falls on the good soil represents noble people with good hearts. They hear Jesus's message, remember it, and produce a crop (tell others).

Some people who hear the message of God's love have it snatched away, others fail to put down roots and grow, and still others allow life to choke out what they heard. However, others hear the word of God and produce a huge harvest.

We all have ears to hear the word of God, but what happens after we hear it?

[Discover more about planting seed in 1 Corinthians 3:6–8.]

21

Are You My Family?

Luke 8:19–21

"My mother and brothers are those who hear God's word and put it into practice."

Luke 8:21

Everyone has parents: a mother and a father. Biologically, that's how we all came into being. And we may have siblings, too, brothers and sisters. Hopefully, our biological parents raised us in a safe, nurturing home. For many of us, our parents are still alive, but for others, one or both parents have passed from this world into the next.

Most people have a relationship with their parents, but not everyone. Maybe the authorities removed them from their biological family to keep them safe. Perhaps some kids ran away. These children may have entered the foster care system or had loving families adopt them. Others remained orphans or became emancipated juveniles.

Regardless of our status now, we are all part of some sort of family—or at least we long to be part of one. Our family may have a biological link, or it may be a group of people who choose to function as a unit. We all need connection. Family is the basis for that bond. This is our physical family.

However, we also have a spiritual family. This one doesn't come from biology but from belief. Our common faith connects us and makes us part of God's family.

Jesus had a physical family too. He had a mother, Mary, and a stepfather, Joseph. He had several brothers—James, Joseph, Simon, and Judas—and multiple sisters, as well as at least one aunt.

Once, as Jesus speaks to a large crowd squeezed into a home, his mother and brothers come to see him. They try to push through the throng, but they can't. There are too many people pressed together to let them through.

However, the crowd passes along word that Jesus's family wants to see him. Someone finally gets the message to Jesus, "Your family is outside and wants to see you."

Jesus doesn't dismiss this news and doesn't stop what he's doing to see them. Instead he uses the situation to instruct the people—and us. He says plainly, "My family are those who hear the word of God and obey it by putting it into practice."

This isn't to disregard his biological heritage. Instead, it reminds us that regardless of the status of our first family—our physical one—we have a second one, too, our spiritual family.

Our human family—whatever that looks like—is essential, as is our spiritual family. May we embrace both as part of God's provision for us.

Do our actions confirm we're part of Jesus's spiritual family?

[Discover more about God's family in Matthew 5:9, Matthew 12:50, John 1:12–13, Romans 8:14–17, and Ephesians 1:4–6.]

22.

A Transfer of Authority
and Power

Luke 9:1–6

*He sent them out to proclaim the kingdom of
God and to heal the sick.*

Luke 9:2

When I think of Jesus's disciples, I envision them following him everywhere he goes. While this happens most of the time, sometimes he sends them out for special tasks. Perhaps the most important of these projects occurs when he dispatches all twelve for a short-term missionary trip. Here's the story:

Jesus calls his twelve disciples. He transfers to them his supernatural power. Then he gives them authority to heal people from their physical maladies and drive out demons. This empowers the disciples to serve others just like Jesus.

Now equipped for ministry, he sends them out. Their mission has two tasks. They're to tell others about God's kingdom, and they're to heal the sick. Today, we understand the telling others about Jesus part, but we mostly ignore the healing others part. Jesus wants his disciples to do both. This suggests he wants us to do both too.

Jesus intends for them to use more than just words to *tell* others about the kingdom of God. He wants them to *show* the power of God's kingdom.

Their words serve as a starting point. However, without tangible evidence, their message is little more than talk. But when the disciples heal others from their diseases and cast out evil spirits, they demonstrate God's power. These actions add substance to their words. This gets people's attention and causes them to seriously consider the disciples' message.

However, before they go, Jesus gives them one more instruction. From a human standpoint, it seems ill-advised. He says, "Don't take anything with you on your journey." Aside from him passing on his power and authority to them, they need no other preparation.

There's merit for embarking on a task and trusting God to provide what we need along the way. Sometimes we must do this, for it's our only option. However, before we turn this into an example to follow in all circumstances, let's fast-forward a bit.

After Jesus eats his final meal with his disciples, he recalls this time when he sent them out to teach and to heal. He reminds them that they took nothing with them. "And what did you lack?"

"Nothing," they say.

Now Jesus gives them a different instruction. He tells them to prepare for what is to happen next: to take provisions and to plan.

It seems that when we follow Jesus, there's a time to move forward in faith that he'll provide what we need. However, there's also a time when we should prepare and plan. May we wisely discern the difference.

Which is easier, to not plan and trust God or to plan and still trust God despite our preparations?

[Discover more about this account in Luke 22:35–36. Read about God giving us what we need in Matthew 6:31–33.]

23.

Who Is Jesus?

Luke 9:18–27

"But what about you?" he asked. "Who do you say I am?" Peter answered, "God's Messiah."

Luke 9:20

J esus asks his disciples an interesting question, "Who do people say I am?"

This is an easy question that they don't have to think about. They quickly give him the top three answers.

"Some say you're John the Baptist," says one.

"Others say you are the incarnation of Elijah," adds another.

A third disciple offers a third view, that Jesus is "one of the ancient prophets who has come back to life."

Having now covered what the masses say about him, Jesus zeroes in on the disciples' perspective. "Now, what do *you* say?" he asks pointedly. "Who do you think I am?"

Peter answers first. Though often impetuous, this time his words are profound. "You are the Messiah, whom God promised to send."

Jesus affirms Peter's answer. Then he does something strange. He begs them not to tell anyone.

Why would Jesus say this?

If he wants to get the word out about the kingdom of God, wouldn't he want his disciples to tell everyone who he is? How can he advance his cause if people hold misconceptions about him? Being an updated version of John the Baptist, Elijah, or another ancient prophet hurts the truth that he is the Messiah, the Savior of the people.

However, should the word get out that Jesus is the Messiah, the Romans could view him as a threat and prematurely execute him for sedition or inciting a rebellion. Though Jesus knows his death will come, it must happen at a different time and through different events. That's why he wants his disciples to keep quiet about this for now.

Thinking about his future, Jesus tells his disciples what's going to happen. He will suffer much. The religious leaders will reject him and see to his execution. But there's good news, too, because three days later he will rise from the dead and live again.

Then he reminds them that they—and by extension, us—need to live a life of self-denial and follow him. "If you want to save your life, you'll lose it," he says, "but if you give up your life for me, you'll save it." Then he warns them not to pursue worldly things at the expense of their spiritual future.

"If you are ashamed of me and the things I say," Jesus adds, "I'll be ashamed of you after you die." Then he adds a curious promise. "Some of you won't die until you first see the kingdom of God."

Who do we say Jesus is? Are we willing to admit it or are we ashamed?

[Discover more in the parallel accounts of this story in Matthew 16:13–20 and Mark 8:27–30.]

Dig Deeper:

The Miracles of Jesus

*"Jesus of Nazareth was a man accredited by
God to you by miracles, wonders and signs."*

Acts 2:22

Luke records over two dozen miracles and supernatural acts that Jesus performed. Though we've covered some of them, we skipped many more. Here's the complete list of what Luke records:

- Jesus drives out a demon, an impure spirit, Luke 4:31–37.

- Jesus heals Simon's mother-in-law, Luke 4:38–39.

- Jesus heals many people and casts out demons, Luke 4:40–41.

- Jesus provides a large catch of fish, Luke 5:4–7.

- Jesus heals a man with leprosy and gives a startling command, Luke 5:12–15.

- Jesus heals a paralytic and forgives him, Luke 5:17–26.

- Jesus heals the man with a shriveled hand, Luke 6:6–11.

- Jesus heals many more people, Luke 6:17–19.

- Jesus heals the Centurion's servant, Luke 7:2–10.

- Jesus raises a widow's son, Luke 7:12–17.

- Jesus cures many who have diseases, sicknesses, and evil spirits, Luke 7:21.

- Jesus cures women of evil spirits and diseases, including Mary Magdalene, Luke 8:2.

- Jesus calms the storm, Luke 8:23–25.

- Jesus heals a demon-possessed man from Gerasenes, Luke 8:26–39.

- Jesus resurrects a dead girl, Luke 8:41–42 and Luke 8:49–56.

- Jesus heals a woman from severe bleeding, Luke 8:43–48.

- Jesus feeds 5,000 people, Luke 9:12–17.

- Jesus heals a boy with an evil spirit, Luke 9:37–43.

- Jesus drives out a demon, Luke 11:14.

- Jesus heals a crippled woman on the Sabbath, Luke 13:10–17.

- Jesus heals a man with edema (swelling), Luke 14:1–4.

- Jesus heals ten lepers, but only one thanks him, Luke 17:12–19.

- Jesus restores a man's sight, Luke 18:35–43.

- Jesus restores a man's ear, after one of his followers cut it off, Luke 22:50–51.

- Jesus vanishes, Luke 24:31.

- Jesus appears among them, Luke 24:36.

- Jesus rises into heaven, Luke 24:51.

How should the miracles and supernatural work of Jesus inform us today? Just as he gave his disciples the authority to heal and cast out demons in his name, can we do the same?

[Discover more about miracles in Acts 19:11, 2 Corinthians 12:12, Galatians 3:5, and Hebrews 2:4.]

24.

See the Kingdom of God

Luke 9:28–36

"This is my Son, whom I have chosen."

Luke 9:35

Eight days after Jesus said some of his disciples wouldn't die until they saw the kingdom of God, we perhaps see his promise play out.

Jesus takes his three main followers, Peter, John, and James, on an outing. They go up a mountain to pray. We can only guess what this prayer time might look like. Is Jesus praying as the disciples listen? Are they all in individual, silent prayer? Or might they take turns praying out loud? Regardless of how these prayers occur, a glorious, supernatural manifestation happens.

As Jesus prays, his appearance changes. His face glows. His garments blaze as bright as a lightning flash. What a magnificent, awe-inspiring, and frightening image.

But there's more. Two men appear next to Jesus. It's Moses and Elijah. They also shine brightly, like Jesus.

Peter, James, and John had been sleepy during their prayer time, perhaps in a spiritual trance. But with Jesus aglow, and Moses and Elijah making a surprise visit, suddenly the three disciples are very much awake.

Jesus, Moses, and Elijah begin talking with each other. They discuss what Jesus will soon do, departing from Earth and fulfilling what the prophets predicted.

Then the conversation ends.

Moses and Elijah prepare to leave and return to the supernatural realm. Peter, likely desperate to capture this moment and the incredible event he just witnessed, blurts out the first thing he thinks. "This is so cool. Let's make three shrines, one for each of you."

Jesus doesn't respond.

A cloud envelops them. If the disciples weren't already frightened, now they surely are. A voice comes from the cloud. It's the voice of God. He says, "This is my boy. I picked him for you. Listen to what he says."

Then the three disciples find themselves alone with Jesus. Moses and Elijah are gone.

This isn't the first time, however, that God speaks out loud about Jesus. As we covered in chapter 9, after John baptizes Jesus, they also hear God's voice. The message of affirmation is similar. "You're my boy. I love you. And I'm most pleased with you."

Peter, James, and John have just witnessed a grand, supernatural event. Is this what Jesus meant when he said some of his disciples would see the kingdom of God before they died?

If God spoke about us, what might he say?

[Discover more about the kingdom of God in Luke 17:20–21, Acts 1:3, and Romans 14:17.]

Dig Deeper:

No Turning Back

"No one who puts a hand to the plow and looks back is fit for service in the kingdom of God."

Luke 9:62

Another time, Jesus says, "No one who looks back when they're plowing is worthy to serve in God's kingdom."

Most of us have never plowed a field, but anyone who has knows that looking behind will cause them to plow a crooked path. The only way to plow a straight line is to look straight ahead, with eyes fixed on where they're going, not where they've been.

Jesus wants his disciples to look straight ahead, keeping their eyes on him. When they look at what's behind, they'll get off course and fail.

Do we look at what's ahead or behind?

[Discover more about looking back in Genesis 19:26.]

25.

Love Your Neighbor

Luke 10:25–37

"'Love the Lord your God with all your heart and with all your soul and with all your strength and with all your mind'; and, 'Love your neighbor as yourself.'"

Luke 10:27

We call one of Jesus's more beloved teachings the Parable of the Good Samaritan. While the name for this parable comes from its main character, a better name is the Parable of Loving Your Neighbor.

Our story starts, like many of them do, with someone coming to Jesus to test him. The person is an expert in the law. Today we might call him a theologian. Let that sink in.

This person doesn't have a genuine question for Jesus. Instead he seeks to make Jesus look bad and himself look good. Despite this, he poses a good question. He asks, "What must I do to receive life eternal?" Who doesn't want to know the answer to that?

As is often the case, Jesus responds to the question with another question. He asks the man, "What does the Law of Moses say about it?"

The theologian is ready with an answer. He says, "Love God totally, and then love your neighbor as much as you care for yourself."

"Correct," Jesus says. These two actions smartly summarize the Law of Moses. "Now, go do this and live."

The theologian squirms. He knows he falls short. He seeks a way out, a loophole to justify his unloving behavior. "Well," he says, "who is my neighbor, anyway?"

Jesus responds with his famous parable of The Good Samaritan. Here's a condensed version: a man gets beat up, robbed, and left to die. A priest—a religious VIP—walks by but doesn't check on the injured guy. A Levite—another religious person—passes by and doesn't help either. A Samaritan—a race despised by most Jews—sees the man and has compassion on him. At risk of also being robbed and beaten, the Samaritan invests his time and money to care for the injured man and make sure he'll be all right.

Then Jesus asks the theologian, "Which of these three men was a good neighbor?"

Unwilling to say "Samaritan" out loud, the theologian merely mumbles, "The one who showed mercy."

Jesus says, "Go and do the same."

The theologian must be in dismay. His plan backfired, and he's embarrassed.

Here are the key points.

First, Jesus confirms the way to eternal life is to love God and love our neighbors.

Second, the definition of neighbor is quite broad. It means everyone.

Third, the star of the story, the one with the right behavior, comes from a race the Jews look down on. He's an outsider, an outcast. The hero is a nobody. This should encourage everyone who doesn't fit in with religious institutions' or society's expectations. That means me, and it may mean you.

Is loving God and loving our neighbors enough to be right with God? How can we love our neighbors as God intends?

[Discover more about love in Leviticus 19:18, Deuteronomy 6:5, and 1 John 4:7–8.]

Dig Deeper:

Holy Spirit Power

Do not cast me from your presence or take your Holy Spirit from me.

Psalm 51:11

Luke mentions the Holy Spirit or Spirit sixteen times in his biography of Jesus. We've already covered some of these passages. Here's the complete list.

- The Holy Spirit fills John the Baptist, even before he's born, Luke 1:15.

- The Holy Spirit impregnates the Virgin Mary, Luke 1:35.

- The Holy Spirit fills Elizabeth, Luke 1:41.

- The Holy Spirit fills Zechariah, Luke 1:67.

- The Holy Spirit is in Simeon, Luke 2:25.

- The Holy Spirit reveals supernatural truth to Simeon, Luke 2:26.

- The Holy Spirit tells Simeon what to do, Luke 2:27.

- John the Baptist says Jesus will baptize with the Holy Spirit and fire, Luke 3:16.

- The Holy Spirit descends on Jesus, Luke 3:22.

- Jesus is full of the Holy Spirit, Luke 4:1.

- Jesus travels under the power of the Holy Spirit, Luke 4:14.

- Jesus reads from Isaiah that the Spirit of God will be upon the Messiah, Luke 4:18 (and Isaiah 61:1–2).

- The Holy Spirit fills Jesus with joy, Luke 10:21.

- Father God will give the Holy Spirit to all who ask, Luke 11:13.

- Blasphemy against the Holy Spirit is unforgiveable, Luke 12:10.

- The Holy Spirit will tell us what to say, Luke 12:12.

How does the Holy Spirit work in us and through us today?

[Discover more about the Holy Spirit, our Advocate, in John 14:26 and John 15:26.]

26

Priorities Matter

Luke 10:38–42

"You are worried and upset about many
things, but few things are needed."

Luke 10:41–42

Jesus and his disciples travel to the village where Martha and her sister, Mary, live. Martha invites them to her home. They accept and drop by to hang out and enjoy some tasty food.

Martha gets busy making a meal, but sister Mary doesn't help. Instead, Mary wants to hear everything Jesus says. She sits at his feet, listening intently. This ticks off Martha. She asks Jesus to make Mary help.

This seems fair, doesn't it? Or is it?

It was Martha's idea to invite Jesus and his team to her home. It was her plan to feed them. Though

Martha may have assumed Mary would agree to help, that was unfair of Martha. Just because she had this generous idea to do something for Jesus, doesn't mean Mary has to go along with it.

Mary has her own plan. She wants to spend time with Jesus. She's doing her thing, while Martha does hers.

Now that's fair.

Martha begs Jesus to make Mary help, which seems perfectly logical from Martha's point of view. But Jesus does the unexpected. I imagine a slight smile appears on his face as he shakes his head. "Martha, Martha, Martha." He laughs gently. "You worry about many things and are worked up over something that isn't that important. Only one thing truly matters. That's what Mary is doing: hanging out with me. I won't take that from her."

How often do we do this ourselves? We have this grand idea to do something for Jesus, and we assume others will join us and help. But we never ask them. We just expect they'll like our idea as much as we do and will work just as hard to make it happen.

Sometimes we make these false assumptions about our spouse or family. Other times we do this with our friends. But the worst is when we do it to the staff at church, especially our pastors. We assume that since we're doing something noble for the kingdom of God, that everyone else will race to help us. After all, it's for a worthy cause.

But God may be inviting these other people—our family, friends, and pastors— into something else. If they stop what they're doing to help us, they're not doing what God wants them to do. And that's not good.

Martha makes food for Jesus, while Mary listens to him. He affirms Mary's choice and dismisses Martha's as secondary. Sometimes, we do things for Jesus that we think are important, but we miss out on something even more worthy. Jesus knew what mattered most, and Mary knew, too, but Martha needed Jesus to help her prioritize.

Are the things we do for Jesus the best things? Are we missing what's truly important?

[Discover more about what's important to God in Hosea 6:6 and Matthew 6:33.]

27.

The Lord's Prayer, Version 2.0

Luke 11:1–13

"Lord, teach us to pray."

Luke 11:1

When Jesus's disciples ask him how to pray, he gives them an example. We call this "The Lord's Prayer." (Though "The Disciples' Prayer" is a better label.) Some people call it the "Our Father" after its opening phrase.

Many people memorize this famous prayer. Have you? Some church traditions recite The Lord's Prayer as part of their worship service. You may be familiar with this as well. You may have learned and recite the version that Matthew includes in his biography of Jesus. It's only sixty-six words long in the New International Version.

Did you know there's another version of The Lord's Prayer? It's in Luke's biography of Jesus. Compared to Matthew's wording, Luke's version omits two phrases and simplifies others. It's even shorter, at only thirty-four words.

Why are there two versions? Did either Matthew or Luke get the words wrong? Or maybe Jesus teaches different versions depending on the needs of his audience. Perhaps there are many variations of this prayer, but we only have two in the Bible.

I've never heard anyone use Luke's version. But it's in the Bible and is worth considering. However, it doesn't matter which version we recite, because I don't think Jesus intended us to memorize it. Instead we should use it as a model to form our own prayers.

There are five main parts to Luke's version:

- Praise God.
- May your kingdom come soon.
- Give us what we need today.
- Forgive our sins, as we forgive others.
- Keep us away from temptation.

Notice that there's not even an "Amen" at the end.

After Jesus gives them this short prayer, he launches into a teaching about prayer. Yep, he has a prayer parable. Two of them, in fact.

The first parable is about a man pounding on his neighbor's door at midnight, begging for food to feed a late-arriving guest. Because of his persistence, the neighbor gives him what he wants. Jesus implies we need to be bold and persistent when we pray. Building on this image of a closed door, Jesus tells us we must ask to receive, seek to find, and knock for the door to open.

The other parable is of a father giving his children the food they ask for, instead of something dangerous. If our earthly fathers, who are flawed, still give us good things, so much more will Papa—who is perfect—give us good things when we ask for them. This includes giving us the Holy Spirit.

How should we use The Lord's Prayer?

[Discover more about The Lord's Prayer in Matthew 6:9–13. Read about seeking God in Matthew 7:7–8.]

28:

The Antidote to Worry

Luke 12:22–32

"But seek his kingdom, and these things will be given to you as well."

Luke 12:31

J esus teaches about worry. Specifically, he says *not* to worry.

We aren't to worry about life, about what we eat or wear. I'm sure Jesus's audience then had a much more basic concern about food and clothing than most of us do today. That doesn't mean there aren't starving people in our world now or those who need something to wear, because there are.

However, for many of us, the question of food isn't where we can find something to eat but what to pick. The same goes for clothes. Our concern isn't about covering our bodies but about which items in our overstuffed closet to put on.

However, just because many of us don't worry about food and clothes like people did 2,000 years ago, we still have plenty of things that concern us. It's just that we worry about *other* things. We may worry about getting a job, covering rent, or whether to buy a car. We worry about the future, such as healthcare, retirement, and growing old. Other concerns include wearing what's in style, buying the newest technology, or what others think about us. These are first-world problems. Yet we worry about them all.

Most of the things we worry about will never happen. Some say the percentage of unrealized worries is 85 percent and others 92, up to a high of 99 percent. That's a lot of time wasted with needless worry.

What should we do instead of worrying?

Jesus reminds us that God feeds the birds and clothes the flowers. How much more so will he take care of us and our needs?

As a child I learned that the antidote to worry was prayer. There's certainly truth in this. Why worry when we can pray? However, I've yet to find a single verse in the Bible that lists prayer as the solution to worry.

What Jesus says about worry is, "Pursue the kingdom of God first. Then these other things will follow." Then Jesus tells us to not be afraid, because God is pleased to give us his kingdom.

Instead of worrying, we can trust God to give us what we need when we seek him and his kingdom. That's the antidote to worry.

When confronted with worry, do we wallow in it or pray about it and trust God to take care of us? How can we seek his kingdom?

[Discover more about not worrying in Matthew 6:25–34 and Luke 10:41–42.]

Dig Deeper:

The Parables of Jesus

He told them many things in parables.

Matthew 13:3

L uke records many parables of Jesus. As I learned in Sunday school, "A parable is an earthly story with a heavenly meaning."

Jesus's parables teach us about the kingdom of God. We're part of it and need to do a better job of acting that way since Jesus talks a lot about God's kingdom and he says next to nothing about church. Perhaps we need to consider his teaching on the kingdom of God more seriously to guide our behaviors, attitudes, and priorities—and not focus so much on secondary things.

Some of Jesus's parables appear in two or three of the biographies of Jesus, while other parables appear in just one. Luke records the most parables, followed closely by Matthew. Mark has less, and John doesn't mention any.

Just as with the miracles of Jesus and the appearance of the Holy Spirit, we covered some of his parables but not all of them. Here is a complete list of Jesus's parables in the book of Luke.

- Garments and wineskins, Luke 5:36–39.

- A speck in another person's eye, Luke 6:39–42.

- The wise and foolish builders, Luke 6:46–49.

- The sower, Luke 8:1–15.

- Put a lamp on a stand, Luke 8:16 and Luke 11:33.

- The Good Samaritan, Luke 10:30–37.

- The persistent neighbor, Luke 11:5–8.

- Ask for good gifts, Luke 11:11–13.

- The strong man, Luke 11:21–22.

- The evil spirit looking for rest, Luke 11:24–26.

- The lamp of the body, Luke 11:34–36.

- The rich man who makes a foolish decision, Luke 12:13–21.

- The folly of worry, Luke 12:22–31.

- The importance of being ready, Luke 12:35–48.

- The fruitless fig tree, Luke 13:6–9.

- The mustard seed, Luke 13:18–19.

- Yeast, Luke 13:20–21.

- The narrow door, Luke 13:24–30.

- Don't pick the best seats, Luke 14:7–14.

- The big banquet, Luke 14:15–24.

- Calculate the cost before building a tower, Luke 14:28–30.

- Look at troop strength before going to war, Luke 14:31–33.

- Remain salty, Luke 14:34–35.

- A lost sheep, Luke 15:3–7.

- A lost coin, Luke 15:8–10.

- A lost son, Luke 15:11–32.

- A shrewd manager, Luke 16:1–9.

- The rich man and Lazarus, Luke 16:19–31.

- The persistent widow who receives justice, Luke 18:1–8.

- The Pharisee and tax collector, Luke 18:9–14.

- Ten minas, Luke 19:11–27.

- Evil tenants, Luke 20:9–19.

- The sign of trees sprouting leaves, Luke 21:29–36.

Which parable relates to something you're going through? Which one can inform or reform how we act? What needs to change?

[Discover more about parables in Hosea 12:10, Mark 4:2, and Luke 8:10.]

29

A Narrow Door and Huge Feast

Luke 13:22–30

"People will come from east and west and north and south, and will take their places at the feast in the kingdom of God."

Luke 13:29

As Jesus makes his circuit through the towns around Jerusalem, someone asks, "Will only a few people be saved?"

As he often does, Jesus answers indirectly. "Put all your efforts into entering through the narrow door, because many who try to get in will fail."

Then Jesus builds upon this image of a door. He talks about a house's owner on the inside and people on the outside pounding to get in. When the owner cracks open the door to peek out, the people beg him to let them in.

"But I don't know you," the owner says.

"Sure, you do," the people answer. "Remember, we've hung out and we've told people about you. So, let us in."

The owner shakes his head. "Nope. Don't try to scam me. You're not getting in." Then he slams the door.

These people cry tears of remorse and grind their teeth in distress. The prophets made it in but not them.

The people who expect to enter—who assume it's a sure thing, that they have an inside track—stand forlorn on the outside. They shake their heads in dismay. It's like a bouncer not letting them enter the club. How disconcerting.

Which side of the door will we be on?

Is getting in going to be easy or hard? Do we think we've done the right things only to find we've fallen short? With our eternal future at risk, how should we react to Jesus's analogy?

Before we totally panic, keep reading. Next Jesus says people will flock from all directions to take their place on the inside for the huge feast in God's kingdom.

This is getting confusing. Will few people make it in through the narrow door or will people swarm in to share in a wonderful celebration?

The answer is "Yes."

Consider the context of Jesus's words to his audience, the Jews. These are the folks in the communities he's visiting, and it's one of them who asks the question about how many will be saved. It's the Jews who Jesus warns to strive to enter through the narrow door. But it will be easy-peasy for the Gentiles.

In reading this, Jesus seems to dismiss God's chosen people in favor of everyone else. He's not, but he's warning them to not take their standing with God as a sure thing, to not assume they're automatically in. Just going to synagogue each week and following a bunch of religious rules isn't enough.

Then Jesus adds, "The last will enter first, but the first will enter last." That is, the Gentiles, who were once outsiders, will get in first, but the Jews, who were once insiders, will get in last. But they will get in.

Who do you think you'll see when you get to Jesus's feast in God's kingdom?

[Discover more about entering God's kingdom in Matthew 7:21, Matthew 18:3, and John 3:5.]

30.

Count the Cost of Following Jesus

Luke 14:25–35

"If anyone comes to me and does not hate father and mother, wife and children, brothers and sisters—yes, even their own life—such a person cannot be my disciple."

Luke 14:26

Another time, as Jesus travels, a large crowd trails behind him. He turns to them to talk about what it takes to truly follow him and be his disciple.

In doing so, Jesus uses some strong language. He uses the word hate.

He says that if we want to be his disciple—a true disciple—we must hate our parents, our spouse, our children, and our siblings. We must even hate our own life. Then he says we should pick up our cross and follow him.

What does he mean about picking up our cross? He's building upon his prior thought about hating our own life. In his day, prisoners dragged their cross through the city on their way to the execution site. For his followers to do this would confirm their allegiance to him and their willingness to die. That's commitment.

These are some serious barriers to deal with. Does Jesus really want us to hate our family and despise our own life to the point of death before we can fully follow him?

No.

Jesus uses exaggeration to make his point. He wants disciples who will make him their priority. He wants disciples to consider what it will cost to follow him. They must commit fully.

He shares two short parables to explain.

The first is a builder who wants to erect a tower. Before he starts, he figures out the total cost of the project. This will save him embarrassment from starting construction and not having enough money to finish. So, too, when we decide to follow Jesus.

The second is a king about to go into battle. Won't he first analyze the situation and look at troop strength to see if he can hope to defeat his enemy? And if he doesn't expect to win, wouldn't he pursue a peaceful solution instead of fighting?

Jesus doesn't want us to say we'll follow him and be his disciples if we don't really mean it, if we haven't considered what it will take to go all in for him. He's not trying to talk us out of it, but he wants us to contemplate what it may cost us to put him first in our lives. First over everything else.

Though we may say we put Jesus first, do our actions confirm it?

[Discover more about following Jesus in Luke 9:23 and Luke 9:57–62.]

31.

Jesus Warns of His Death

Luke 18:31–34

"Everything that is written by the prophets about the Son of Man will be fulfilled."

Luke 18:31

J esus knows he'll die soon. He pulls his twelve disciples aside for a private lesson. He tells them plainly what will happen. But this isn't the first time he does this. It's the third.

The first occurs after Peter boldly proclaims that Jesus is the Messiah, sent from God. Peter affirms Jesus's pedigree and his mission. Not only does Peter get it right, but the other disciples hear him. Now they all know.

How this must encourage Jesus. Finally his disciples are beginning to understand who he is and what he'll do. This is a fitting time for him to be direct and explain things in detail. Right after Peter proclaims Jesus as the Messiah, Jesus explains what will happen. "I'll suffer much, the religious leaders will reject me, and then I'll be killed. But three days later I'll come back to life."

Luke doesn't record the disciples' reactions to this shocking news. Perhaps it's because the disciples don't react. Maybe Jesus's words are so foreign to them that they don't know what to make of it or what to say. So they say nothing.

The second time Jesus brings up the subject happens a few days later. He's just healed a boy with an evil spirit, and the people marvel at God's power. His disciples are likely in awe too. Jesus turns to them. "Listen up," he says. "I have something important to tell you. I'm going to be betrayed and handed over to the authorities for execution."

They still don't get it, but they're afraid to ask what he means.

Having tried twice—and failed—to let his disciples know what will happen, Jesus gives it a third try. Surely they'll understand now. They must. He's running out of time.

"We're going to Jerusalem," he says. "Everything the prophets say about me will happen. The authorities will do terrible things to me, and I'll die. Then three days later I'll come alive again."

The disciples shake their heads. They have no idea what he means, as if he's talking nonsense. It's not that the disciples are stupid. They know what the Scriptures say about the coming Messiah. They should be able to understand, but they don't. They can't connect the dots.

How this must discourage Jesus. He's spent three years with them. And this is the third time he's told them he's going to die. They still don't get it. Maybe they aren't ready after all.

When we receive a new spiritual insight, how many times do we need to hear it before it sinks in?

[Discover more about the other two times Jesus predicted his death in Luke 9:22 and Luke 9:44–45.]

PART 3:

JESUS OVERCOMES DEATH

Luke 19:28 to 24:53

32.

Like a Rock Star

Luke 19:28–40

The whole crowd of disciples began joyfully to praise God in loud voices for all the miracles they had seen.

Luke 19:37

As Jesus and his disciples head toward Jerusalem, he sends two of them on ahead with a curious instruction. "Go into the village," he says, "and there you'll find a colt that has never been ridden. Untie it and bring it to me. If anyone tries to stop you, just say, 'It's for the Lord.'"

Note that there's no promise of returning the animal. It's like they're stealing it. A modern equivalent might be snatching a car. Would you boost a car for Jesus? Would the police believe your explanation?

Yet the disciples do what Jesus says. The people who question their actions accept their story.

The two disciples bring the colt to Jesus, throw their coats on the animal as a makeshift saddle, and then set Jesus upon him. They head off to Jerusalem.

As they go, people stand aside and throw their coats on the road. The whole crowd yells out their praise to God. "Hail the King who comes in God's name," they cheer. "Heavenly peace and great glory," they exclaim. They receive him like we would celebrate a rock star.

It must seem to the disciples as the culmination of three years of preparation. Finally Jesus receives the acclaim he deserves. He rides into Jerusalem as a king. Surely he's going to kick out the Romans, take over the nation, and rule Israel instead of their foreign occupiers. As a direct descendant of David, Jesus will continue the royal line, and everything will be as it should. At least that's how most Jews interpret the words of the prophets.

However, the Pharisees in the crowd are aghast. They tell Jesus to shush his raucous followers. But Jesus won't. He says that even if he did, "the stones would erupt in praise."

The people proclaim Jesus, they celebrate his ride into Jerusalem, and they expect earth-shattering things will happen. Historic things will indeed occur. But it's not what the people assume. It even surprises the twelve disciples.

Does Jesus always live up to our expectations? How do we react when he doesn't?

[Discover more about this event in John 12:13–16.]

Dig Deeper:

Rightly Interpreting Scripture

*They brought it to Jesus, threw their cloaks on
the colt and put Jesus on it.*

Luke 19:35

When Jesus rides into Jerusalem as a king, the people see him as the fulfillment of what the prophets foresaw and extensively wrote about. Jesus will rescue them from foreign oppression, overthrow Roman rule, and ascend to his rightful throne—forever. He will be their king, their promised Savior.

At least that was the conventional interpretation.

They, of course, got it wrong. They looked for a physical king to save them, while God intended to give them a spiritual king.

As long as people read Scripture, some folks will get it wrong.

How willing are we to accept that our understanding of certain Bible passages might be wrong?

[Discover more about studying the Bible in John 5:39–40 and Acts 17:11. Read this prophecy in Zechariah 9:9–10.]

Dig Deeper:

Jesus Weeps

As he approached Jerusalem and saw the city,
he wept over it.

Luke 19:41

As Jesus rides into Jerusalem, he pauses and cries for the city. But this isn't the only time Jesus cries.

John notes that Jesus cries when he stands outside of Lazarus's tomb (John 11:35).

What are the similarities between these two occasions?
Does Jesus ever cry for us?

[Discover more weeping in Jeremiah 9:1.]

33.

Judas Sells Out

Luke 22:1–6

*He consented, and watched for an
opportunity to hand Jesus over to them when
no crowd was present.*

Luke 22:6

L et's take a moment to review.

Jesus has ridden into town in a grand procession, and the people hail him as king, their Savior sent from God. If word gets out, the Romans could view him as a threat and execute him for insurrection—an open revolt against the government. When this happens, it's going to make things even tougher for the Jews. It will threaten what little control the Romans have allowed them to have over their nation.

Next, the masses have flocked to Jesus. The religious leaders see their followers abandoning them and their influence eroding. If they hope to regain their authority over the people, they must stop Jesus. On one side they fear the Romans, and on the other they fear losing what little power they have. They look for a way to get rid of Jesus without incurring the wrath of the people.

Third, Jesus, in predicting his death, says someone will betray him.

In addition, Judas is the treasurer for Jesus's ministry. He carries their money bag. It's not because he's good with money, because he isn't. In fact, he's greedy and helps himself to their funds.

All these things culminate in what happens next. Yet it requires one more element: Satan.

Satan enters Judas Iscariot, one of Jesus's twelve disciples. Satan tempts Judas to go to the religious leaders and discuss what to do about Jesus. Judas is willing to hand him over to them, so they can stop him.

Judas's offer delights the religious leaders, and they agree to pay him for his part in their scheme. The thought of receiving money is all the convincing Judas needs to do the unthinkable. He is going to betray Jesus.

Today, people view Judas in one of three ways.

Some see him as an integral part of God's plan to bring salvation to his people. Without Judas, Jesus wouldn't have died to save us. This makes Judas a helpless cog in God's grand plan.

Others suggest that Judas knew exactly what he was doing. They assert that he and Jesus even planned this to bring about the necessary events for Jesus to die and overcome death. This makes Judas a hero.

Still others see him as a pawn of Satan, unable to control what he did. This makes Judas a victim.

All these are wrong. Judas is not helpless, a hero, or a victim.

The reality is that Satan tempted Judas to do wrong, and he gave in to the temptation. This makes Judas just like us.

In what ways do we betray Jesus?

[Discover more about the religious leaders' opposition to Jesus in Luke 19:47–48. Read about Judas in Matthew 27:3–5, Luke 22:22, and John 12:6.]

34.

The Last Supper is the First Communion

Luke 22:7–20

"Go and make preparations for us to eat the Passover."

Luke 22:8

Moses institutes Passover as a meal eaten just before the people leave Egypt to return to the land God promised for them through Abraham. For this first Passover meal they eat in haste, dressed for a quick departure for a long journey.

With no time for yeast to rise, they eat bread with no leaven in it, as in unleavened bread. For their main course, they dine on roasted lamb. They take blood from the lamb and brush it on their doorpost.

This signals to God to "pass over" their home when he strikes down the firstborn in each family.

To remind them of this first Passover, God wants them to observe this ceremony when they reach the Promised Land. Throughout the centuries, the people repeat Passover as an annual celebration.

Jesus wants to celebrate Passover, the day of unleavened bread, with his disciples—one last time. He sends Peter and John to prepare the meal. They ask, "Where?"

Jesus gives them a curious answer. He tells them that when they get to the city, they'll see a man carrying a jar of water. They're to follow him. He'll enter a home. They should find the owner and say, "The teacher asks, 'Where's the guestroom for him to eat Passover with us?'" Talk about cryptic.

Peter and John obey Jesus, and the owner shows them a room already furnished. There they prepare for the Passover meal.

Later Jesus and his disciples recline at the table to enjoy the Passover feast. He's eager to share this meal with them. It's his last supper.

Jesus starts the meal with a cup of wine in hand and gives thanks to God. He tells them to share it and says he won't drink wine again until the Kingdom of

God comes. Then he breaks the unleavened bread into pieces and passes it to them. This symbolizes the sacrifice he will make with his body.

After the meal he takes another cup of wine. This time he says, "This cup represents a new covenant made with my blood, which I shed for you."

This is the first Communion.

Do we approach Communion in awe over what Jesus did, treat it as a ritual we must complete, or struggle somewhere in between?

[Discover more about the first Passover in Exodus 12:1–28.]

Dig Deeper:

Four Accounts of the Last Supper

"I have eagerly desired to eat this Passover with you before I suffer."

Luke 22:15

We often call the final meal Jesus eats with his disciples, before he's executed, The Last Supper. It's a Passover celebration with some new parts that Jesus adds. Today, we continue this tradition in memory of him.

Though people use different names for it, such as Communion, Holy Communion, The Lord's Supper, The Eucharist, and Holy Eucharist, among others, the intent is the same: remembering what Jesus did for us.

Matthew, Mark, and Luke all record this event in their biographies of Jesus. However, each of them presents it differently. Matthew's version is perhaps most familiar, frequently read during many Communion services. Mark's version is similar, though not used as often.

However, Luke's version is more detailed, with a pre-dinner sacrament using wine and bread, along with a post-dinner salute with wine. At the beginning of the meal, Jesus gives thanks and tells them to share the wine with one another. Then he breaks the bread, referencing his body, which is about to be broken for their salvation. However, it's not until the second use of wine, after the meal, when Jesus refers to the cup as a new covenant signifying his death (his spilt blood), which is for them.

With Luke's version, we can't overlook the fact that an actual meal occurs as part of Communion. This is what most of us miss with our Communion celebrations today. The observance of Communion shouldn't be a tiny cracker and sip of wine. It's a special meal shared in community, all in the name of Jesus.

Later, Paul gives the church in Corinth instructions on celebrating communion. This is the fourth time the Bible talks about communion. Each account gives us valuable insight into this mysterious, wondrous act.

Luke's description about Communion is the most detailed. Should we ignore it or elevate it?

[Discover more about communion in Matthew 26:26–29, Mark 14:22–24, Luke 22:17–20, and 1 Corinthians 11:23–34.]

35.

Two Failures and Two Responses

Luke 22:21–34

But he replied, "Lord, I am ready to go with you to prison and to death."

Luke 22:33

As Jesus shares wine with his disciples to wrap up the meal, he also has some other things to share—dreadful things.

First, Jesus tells his disciples that one of them will betray him. Someone who has just shared this sacred meal with them is going to turn on him and then turn him in. Jesus says this must happen, and it will happen regardless, but a special dose of major woe awaits the man who betrays him.

The disciples can't believe it. Who would do such a thing? I'm sure Judas is just as adamant in his denials as the other eleven.

It doesn't take long for the discussion to turn around from who's the betrayer to who's the best among the twelve. Jesus tells them they have it all wrong. "The greatest should be the least, and the ruler should serve." Then Jesus confirms they will help him rule the twelve tribes of Israel.

After this distraction about who's the most important, Jesus turns to Simon Peter. Jesus knows that Satan wants to take Peter down. Jesus has already prayed that Peter will be strong, that his faith will prevail. Then Peter can rebound from his failure to encourage the others.

Peter says, "I'll never let you down. I'm ready to go to jail and even die for you."

Jesus shakes his head. "Before the rooster crows tomorrow morning, three times you will have disavowed that you even know me."

Jesus understands that Judas will betray him, and that Peter will deny him.

Though Jesus prays that Peter will bounce back from his failure, the Bible records no similar prayer for Judas. And Luke doesn't mention what happens later to Judas or Peter, but Matthew and John do. Through them we know that Judas commits suicide in anguish over his role in bringing about Jesus's death. And we know that Jesus restores Peter back into right relationship with him and the rest of the disciples.

Peter gets a second chance, but Judas doesn't stick around to find out if he will.

We may think we're willing to go to jail and even die for Jesus, but when that moment comes, will we react like Peter?

[Discover more about Judas's and Peter's responses to their failures in Matthew 27:5 and Matthew 26:75.]

Dig Deeper:

Two Swords and One Ear

"See, Lord, here are two swords."

Luke 22:38

After Jesus's final meal with his followers and his warning of betrayal and denial, he tells them to buy swords. His disciples say that they already have two.

Did you catch that? Jesus's disciples carry swords.

I don't know about you, but I've never envisioned Jesus's band of followers as wielding weapons. Although I've seen many paintings of them, along with many more movies, never once did I notice a disciple with a saber strapped to his waist. The whole idea shocks me, yet at a time when Jesus tells them to buy a sword, they already have two.

If I were picking people to start a ministry with, I'd certainly exclude anyone brandishing a blade. Yet

Jesus has different criteria. He accepts his followers as they are: with baggage, failings—and swords.

But there's more. Just a few hours later, Jesus goes out with his disciples to pray. As he finishes, Judas walks up, with a mob in tow. He kisses Jesus.

One of Jesus's disciples eagerly asks, "Shall we fight?" Before Jesus answers, one of the sword-carrying disciples whips out his weapon and slashes at the high priest's servant. Though likely aiming for the guy's head, all the disciple gets is an ear. Even though he doesn't know how to fight, he tries.

This isn't what Jesus meant when he said to go buy swords. "Stop!" he says. He touches the servant's ear and heals him.

Then they arrest Jesus.

Are we willing to fight for Jesus? Is this what he wants?

[Discover more about this incident in Luke 22:47–51 and John 18:10–11.]

36

Jesus's Prayer

Luke 22:39–46

"Father, if you are willing, take this cup from me; yet not my will, but yours be done."

Luke 22:42

The Bible is full of perplexing stories.

One is when God tells Abraham to sacrifice his only son, Isaac. What father would kill his son? What God would demand it?

However, Abraham wants to obey God regardless of the cost.

Three days later we find Abraham on a mountain with his son, Isaac, tied up on an altar. With knife in hand, Abraham raises his arm, ready to plunge the dagger into Isaac's chest. Just then, God stops him. "No!" he says. "Don't do it. It was just a test to see if you would obey me."

Wow, that was close. Then God provides a ram for the sacrifice instead of Isaac. Abraham proves himself faithful to God, and Isaac is spared.

Fast-forward several centuries to Jesus. Before his arrest and execution, Jesus spends time praying. His disciples wait nearby. He tells them to pray so that they won't give in to temptation. We don't know if Jesus had a specific temptation in mind or if this is for them to guard against all kinds of temptation. But we do know that his disciples fall asleep as he prays. Perhaps they longed to close their eyes—just for a minute—but they nod off.

At one point in his prayer, Jesus asks God for a reprieve—that he won't have to die—even though that was the plan all along. But he's quick to add an addendum. He'll do whatever Papa wants.

I wonder if Jesus is thinking about the test God gave Abraham, commanding the patriarch to kill his son, Isaac. For Abraham and Isaac, God the Father says, "Stop!" Then he provides a different sacrifice, a substitute. Isaac gets a reprieve, and the ram dies in his place.

Does Jesus hope God will again say, "Stop! This is just a test" and provide a substitute sacrifice or a different solution? But this time Papa doesn't offer an alternative. Jesus must die as a once-and-for-all sacrifice to restore us into right relationship with Father God.

However, God sends an angel to Jesus to encourage him. Now knowing there's no plan B, Jesus prays in earnest anguish. Sweat falls from him like drops of blood.

When Jesus finishes praying, he finds his disciples asleep. They weren't even able to stay awake and support him in the darkest time of his life. Again he tells them to pray so that they won't give in to temptation. Maybe he's thinking specifically about Peter and Judas.

When it comes to Jesus dying instead of us and taking our punishment on himself, he doesn't have second thoughts, but he is open to alternatives. God doesn't provide one.

Jesus dies to make us right with the Father. Though our wrongs separate us from God, Jesus takes our punishment upon himself, thereby restoring us to right relationship with Papa.

Jesus obeys. Jesus dies. We live.

Do we fight temptation with prayer or give in to it?

[Discover more about God provision of an alternate sacrifice for Isaac in Genesis 22:1–14.]

37.

Personal Agendas Thwart Justice

Luke 22:66 to Luke 23:25

But with loud shouts they insistently demanded that he be crucified, and their shouts prevailed. So Pilate decided to grant their demand.

Luke 23:23–24

The Jewish leaders have arrested Jesus. They did it quietly in the darkness of night, without arousing the anger of his crowd of followers. Phase one is complete. Now on to phase two. They must silence him for good.

In the morning the religious leaders interrogate Jesus. They ask if he's the Messiah. At first he gets philosophical. Next he implies he is. Then they ask him directly, "Are you the Son of God?"

Jesus says, "You say I am."

To the Jewish leaders, Jesus's implication that he's God's Son is enough to condemn him to death for blasphemy. However, their Roman rulers have withheld from them the power to execute people. The Romans reserved crucifixion for themselves. So the Jewish leaders drag Jesus to Pilate, the Romans' local representative.

The Jewish leaders sling various accusations against Jesus. They say he's subverting their nation. False, though they may feel he's subverting their religion.

Next they say he opposes paying taxes. False. In fact, Jesus advocated paying rightful taxes.

Third, they say he claims to be a king. Half true. Though Jesus is king, he never said it.

Pilot dismisses their charges and pronounces Jesus innocent.

But the religious leaders don't give up. They try again. They assert that Jesus's teaching stirs up the people. False. The only people Jesus riled up were the Jewish leaders because he confronted their hypocrisy. The rest of the people embraced Jesus.

At this point, Pilate sees a way out and sends Jesus to Herod.

Herod's excited to meet Jesus. For a long time he's wanted to see Jesus and hopes to witness a miracle. Herod asks many questions, but Jesus doesn't answer. The religious leaders grow agitated and throw more accusations at Jesus. Herod grows bored and starts ridiculing Jesus too. So do his soldiers. After mocking him, they send him back to Pilate.

Pilate again asserts Jesus's innocence. He says he'll punish Jesus and then release him. Why would you punish an innocent man? This isn't justice.

The crowd shouts, "Away with him!"

Pilate wants to release Jesus and begs the crowd to reconsider.

They're not listening. Instead they call for Jesus's execution.

A third time Pilate asserts Jesus's innocence. But he eventually gives in to public pressure because it's an easy solution and a safe way out. So he offers to punish and then release Jesus.

But the people keep shouting. A mob mentality erupts, so Pilate gives in to their demands and allows the Romans to execute Jesus.

The Jewish leaders don't care about what is right. They have their own agenda. And though Herod could've done something to protect Jesus, he does nothing.

Are we willing to pursue justice at all costs, or do we take the easy way out in the face of opposition?

[Discover more about Pilate trying to release Jesus in Matthew 27:22–26 and Mark 15:9–15.]

Dig Deeper:

The Old Testament Cited in Luke

Then Jesus said to them, "Why is it said that the Messiah is the son of David?"

Luke 20:41

The book of Luke includes twenty-three references to passages in the Old Testament. There are five each from Deuteronomy, Psalms, and Isaiah. In some cases Jesus quotes them, and in other instances Luke weaves them into his narrative.

- Luke 2:23 refers to Exodus 13:2 and 12.

- Luke 2:24 refers to Leviticus 12:8.

- Luke 3:6 refers to Isaiah 40:3–5.

- Luke 4:4 refers to Deuteronomy 8:3.

- Luke 4:8 refers to Deuteronomy 6:13.

- Luke 4:11 refers to Psalm 91:11–12.

- Luke 4:12 refers to Deuteronomy 6:16.

- Luke 4:19 refers to Isaiah 61:1–2.

- Luke 7:27 refers to Malachi 3:1.

- Luke 8:10 refers to Isaiah 6:9.

- Luke 10:27 refers to Deuteronomy 6:5.

- Luke 10:27 also refers to Leviticus 19:18.

- Luke 13:35 refers to Psalm 118:26.

- Luke 18:20 refers to Exodus 20:12–16.

- Luke 18:20 also refers to Deuteronomy 5:16–20.

- Luke 19:38 refers to Psalm 118:26.

- Luke 19:46 refers to Isaiah 56:7.

- Luke 19:46 also refers to Jeremiah 7:11.

- Luke 20:17 refers to Psalm 118:22.

- Luke 20:37 refers to Exodus 3:6.

- Luke 20:43 refers to Psalm 110:1.

- Luke 22:37 refers to Isaiah 53:12.

- Luke 23:30 refers to Hosea 10:8.

How can the Old Testament inform our understanding of the New Testament . . . and of God?

[Discover more about connecting the Old Testament to Jesus in Matthew 26:54.]

38

Two Responses to Punishment

Luke 23:39–43

*"Truly I tell you, today you will be with
me in paradise."*

Luke 23:43

When the Romans execute Jesus, they crucify two criminals with him, one on either side. While we don't know what these men did to deserve the death penalty, we can assume it must have been something serious, such as murder or insurrection.

One of the criminals mocks Jesus, but the other one doesn't. Instead, this second criminal rebukes the first. He says, "Knock it off. We're guilty and getting what we deserve, but this guy is innocent." The criminal knows the punishment for him and the other lawbreaker is just. They're getting what their actions warrant, whereas Jesus isn't.

Then, in an amazing display of faith—since they will all soon be dead—the second criminal asks Jesus to remember him in his future kingdom. This simple request to Jesus carries with it a confidence that there's a future after death, and that Jesus has the power to grant this plea.

This man, whose life is about to end because of a serious wrong he committed, knows something awaits him after his final breath. Yet through no merit of his own, and with nothing he can do to earn it, the criminal asks to be part of Jesus's future kingdom. It's sincere, and it's bold.

Jesus could have said, "Sorry, man. You messed up. It's too late." Instead he says, "No problem." And not only is the answer positive, it's also imminent. Jesus adds, "Today you will be with me in paradise." It's a done deal.

How cool is that?

Just like these two criminals, we, too, have sinned. Regardless of how minor or severe our mistakes, our actions deserve the same punishment: death. Yet through Jesus, we can receive mercy. If we turn to him and admit our mistakes, he'll grant us a reprieve, and we can spend eternity with him in paradise.

While we could wait until the last minute and make a deathbed conversion with full confidence that Jesus will say, "Yes," the risk is too high. We don't know when our last breath will come or if we'll have time to ask Jesus to remember us.

Don't put it off. We must all admit our faults to Jesus today, so we can live for him on earth in this life and live with him in paradise in the next.

There are many ideas about what we must do to be saved, but for this criminal, Jesus made it easy. Are we willing to accept this?

[Discover more about salvation in Romans 3:21–24, Romans 10:9–13, and 1 John 1:9.]

39.

Jesus's Death and Burial

Luke 23:44–56

Going to Pilate, [Joseph] asked for Jesus' body.
Then he took it down, wrapped it in linen
cloth and placed it in a tomb.

Luke 23:52–53

As Jesus hangs on the cross, his life ebbs away. Minute by minute he moves toward death, in one of the most agonizing ways possible. Then in the middle of the day, everything goes dark. It stays that way for three hours. Luke writes that the sun stops shining.

Some people explain this as an eclipse, but given its length, it must be a supernatural event. Regardless, it's unexpected and unusual. Unprecedented, it certainly grabs the people's attention. Then the curtain in the temple that separates the holiest place from the common people, rips apart. Symbolically, all people now have direct access to God. Then Jesus dies.

The centurion overseeing the crucifixion has never seen anything like this. He knows what death looks like, for he has seen many. He knows Jesus is dead. The centurion senses God's power in what happened, praises God, and affirms Jesus as a righteous man.

The people watching the crucifixion are overcome by what they just saw. Jesus is dead. They hang their heads in sorrow and walk away. Jesus's friends, including some of his female followers, stand at a distance, watching all this take place.

The Roman centurion, the people in the crowd, and Jesus's followers all witness his death. All that remains is to bury him.

Joseph—a member of the religious council which brought about Jesus's death—didn't agree with the decision to kill him. A man of integrity, hailing from the town of Arimathea, he lives in expectation of the coming kingdom of God. Joseph goes to Pilate and asks for Jesus's body to give him a proper burial.

Joseph must act fast, for the Sabbath is about to start, and his faith keeps him from work on this holy day. He takes down Jesus's body, wraps it in linen, and places it in a new tomb, one hewn from rock. Then a huge stone is placed at the entrance to seal the crypt. This marks the certainty of Jesus's death.

The women who watched Jesus die follow Joseph and see him place Jesus's lifeless body in the tomb. Then they head home to gather spices, so they can embalm his body. But since they can't do it on the Sabbath, they must wait until the first day of the week to perform this loving act for their fallen Savior.

Jesus is dead, and his body lies in a tomb. Many eyewitnesses confirm his death and his burial. They assume this is the end.

Do we sometimes forget the significance of Jesus's death and how much he suffered so that we could live?

[Discover what Isaiah predicted about how Jesus would suffer in Isaiah 52:14 and Isaiah 53:4–6.]

40

Eyewitnesses to the Resurrected Jesus

Luke 24:1–43

"It is true! The Lord has risen and has appeared to Simon."

Luke 24:34

Jesus is dead and buried, but this isn't the end. In many ways it's the beginning. After being dead for three days, Jesus resurrects. He has overcome the finality of death.

As they planned, on the first day of the week, the women who had prepared spices to embalm Jesus head to his tomb. When they arrive, someone has moved the stone that blocked the entrance. They go inside, expecting to see Jesus's body, but it's not there.

Suddenly two angels appear. They say, "Why do you seek someone who's living in a place for the dead? He is alive! Don't you remember what he said?" Then the women recall Jesus's words, and everything begins to make sense. They hurry to tell the other disciples, but they don't believe the women.

However, Peter runs to check things out. He finds the tomb empty just like the women said. He wonders what happened.

Later in the day, two of Jesus's followers walk down the road to the village of Emmaus. On their journey, Jesus joins them, but they don't recognize him. He listens as they talk about him. He pretends to not know what they're discussing and asks them to explain. Eagerly they do.

After they tell him about the hoped-for Savior who was executed, Jesus begins teaching them. He connects Old Testament prophecy with how he just fulfilled it. When the pair reaches their destination, they ask Jesus to stay with them. He does.

At the meal Jesus breaks the bread, thanks God, and passes it to them. At last they recognize him. But then he disappears. The pair remark about how he deeply touched their hearts and engaged their minds as he taught them from the Hebrew Scriptures.

They race back to Jerusalem to tell everyone that they saw and talked to Jesus. He's alive! They get to Jerusalem and find the remaining eleven disciples, but before the two can say a thing, the disciples have news for them. "Jesus has arisen, and he appeared to Peter."

As they talk, Jesus materializes in the room. Though they're afraid and confused, Jesus speaks to them and proves he's alive.

He's alive. Jesus is alive. This changes everything.

If we saw Jesus today, would we recognize him? When we see him at work, do we acknowledge it?

[Discover more about Jesus rising from the dead in Acts 5:30, 1 Corinthians 15:20–23, and 2 Timothy 1:10.]

Dig Deeper:

A Frustrating Verse

*And beginning with Moses and all the
Prophets, he explained to them what was said
in all the Scriptures concerning himself."*

Luke 24:27

There's a verse in the Bible that frustrates me—
not for what it says, but for what it doesn't say.

As Jesus walks with the pair headed to
Emmaus, he reminds them what the Bible says about
him. But Luke doesn't record what Jesus says.

This irritates me. I want to know. I long to read
exactly what Jesus said. Give me details. Quote the
passages and include Jesus's explanation.

True, there are a limited number of verses in the
Old Testament that point to Jesus, so we could study
them and guess which ones he picked. But speculat-
ing about these verses isn't enough.

Next, what did Jesus say about these passages? I yearn to know which verses Jesus cited and hear him explain them. Anything short of that leaves me wanting more.

Is longing for more of Jesus a good thing? How should we handle this?

[Discover more about the things not recorded about Jesus in John 21:25.]

Dig Deeper:

Their Eyes Are Opened

Then their eyes were opened and they recognized him.

Luke 24:31

As Cleopas and his friend walk to the village of Emmaus, Jesus joins them. They don't recognize him. Jesus explains what the Scriptures predict about him. Fascinated by what he shares, they invite him to supper. During the meal, their eyes are opened, and they realize it's Jesus.

This idea of people's eyes being opened also occurs much earlier in the Bible, in Genesis. As soon as Adam and Eve do precisely what God told them not to do, their eyes are also opened—and they realize they're naked.

Just as our eyes can open to the knowledge that we don't measure up to God's standard, our eyes can also open to Jesus as the solution.

Are our eyes open to see Jesus?

[Discover more about Adam and Eve having their eyes opened in Genesis 3:7. Read this passage in Luke 24:13–35.]

Epilogue:

A Special Gift

Luke 24:48–53

"I am going to send you what my Father has promised; but stay in the city until you have been clothed with power from on high."

Luke 24:49

L et's recap: Jesus died and was buried. He rose from the dead and appeared to his followers.

They're his witnesses. It's up to them to continue what he started.

It's time for him to leave our world and return to heaven. But before he goes, he has some exciting news to share. He's going to send them a present, a special gift that Papa promises to give them.

What is this gift? When will it arrive? Jesus doesn't say, but he does tell them to wait for it in Jerusalem.

He leads them out of the city. With hands raised, he blesses them. As he does, his body levitates. He rises into heaven.

With much joy they return to Jerusalem and worship him. They stay in the temple praising God as they wait to receive their special gift.

To be continued . . .

Jesus has a special gift for us too. Have we received it?

[Discover more about God's special gift in Acts 1:4–5 and Acts 2:4.]

The story of Jesus and his special gift continues in the book of Acts in the Bible. And it continues in this book's sequel, *Tongues of Fire: 40 Devotional Insights for Today's Church from the Book of Acts.*

For Small Groups

That You May Know makes an ideal eight-week discussion guide for small groups. In preparation for the conversation, read one chapter of this book each weekday, Monday through Friday.

Week 1: Read 1 through 5.

Week 2: Read 6 through 10.

Week 3: Read 11 through 15.

Week 4: Read 16 through 20.

Week 5: Read 21 through 25.

Week 6: Read 26 through 30.

Week 7: Read 31 through 35.

Week 8: Read 36 through 40.

Then, when you get together in your small group, discuss the questions at the end of each chapter. The leader can guide this discussion for all the questions or pick some to focus on.

Before beginning the discussion, pray as a group. Ask for Holy Spirit insight and clarity.

Then, while considering each chapter's questions:

- Look for how this can grow your understanding of the Bible.

- Evaluate how this can expand your faith perspective.

- Consider what you need to change in how you live your lives.

- Ask God to help you apply what you've learned.

May God speak to you as you use this book to study his Word and grow closer to him.

Bonus Content:

If You're New to the Bible

E ach entry in this book contains Bible references. These can guide you if you want to learn more. If you're not familiar with the Bible, here's a brief overview to get you started, give some context, and minimize confusion.

First, the Bible is a collection of works written by various authors over several centuries. Think of the Bible as a diverse anthology of godly communication. It contains historical accounts, poetry, songs, letters of instruction and encouragement, messages from God sent through his representatives, and prophecies.

Most versions of the Bible have sixty-six books grouped into two sections: The Old Testament and the New Testament. The Old Testament contains thirty-nine books that precede and anticipate Jesus. The New Testament includes twenty-seven books and covers Jesus's life and the work of his followers.

The reference notations in the Bible, such as Romans 3:23, are analogous to line numbers in a Shakespearean play. They serve as a study aid. Since the Bible is much longer and more complex than a play, its reference notations are more involved.

As already mentioned, the Bible is an amalgam of books, or sections, such as Genesis, Psalms, John, Acts, or 1 Peter. These are the names given to them, over time, based on the piece's author, audience, or purpose.

In the 1200s, each book was divided into chapters, such as Acts 2 or Psalm 23. In the 1500s, the chapters were further subdivided into verses, such as John 3:16. Let's use this as an example.

The name of the book (John) is first, followed by the chapter number (3), a colon, and then the verse number (16). Sometimes called a chapter-verse reference notation, this helps people quickly find a specific text regardless of their version of the Bible.

Here's how to look up a specific passage in the Bible based on its reference: Most Bibles contain a table of contents, which gives the page number for the beginning of each book. Start there. Locate the book you want to read, and turn to that page number. Then page forward to find the chapter you want. Last, skim that page to locate the specific verse.

If you want to read online, just pop the entire reference, such as 2 Timothy 3:16, into a search engine, and you'll get lots of links to online resources. You can also go directly to BibleGateway.com or use the YouVersion app.

Although the goal was to place these chapter and verse divisions at logical breaks, they sometimes seem arbitrary. Therefore, it's a good practice to read what precedes and follows each passage you're studying since the text before or after it may contain relevant insight into the portion you're exploring.

Learn more about the greatest book ever written at ABibleADay.com, which provides a Bible blog, summaries of the books of the Bible, a dictionary of Bible terms, Bible reading plans, and other resources.

Acknowledgments

I sincerely acknowledge:

God for giving me the desire to write, the ability to do so, and the inspiration for what to write about.

My patient wife who gives me the time and space to write.

The members of Kalamazoo Christian Writers for encouragement and support.

Shara Anjaynith Cazon for doing some of my other work so I can write more.

James L. Rubart for encouraging me to push through the things I don't like to do when it comes to promoting my books.

Joanna Penn for teaching me about writing and publishing through her podcast each week.

And I'm especially grateful for each person who invested forty days to read this book. May God bless you and encourage you through these words.

About Peter DeHaan

Peter DeHaan, PhD, wants to change the world one word at a time. His books and blog posts discuss God, the Bible, and church, geared toward spiritual seekers and church dropouts. Many people feel church has let them down, and Peter seeks to encourage them as they search for a place to belong.

But he's not afraid to ask tough questions or make religious people squirm. He's not trying to be provocative. Instead, he seeks truth, even if it makes people uncomfortable. Peter urges Christians to push past the status quo and reexamine how they practice their faith in every part of their lives.

Peter earned his doctorate, awarded with high distinction, from Trinity College of the Bible and Theological Seminary. He lives with his wife in beautiful Southwest Michigan and wrangles crossword puzzles in his spare time.

A lifelong student of Scripture, Peter wrote the 700-page website ABibleADay.com to encourage people to explore the Bible, the greatest book ever written. His popular blog, at PeterDeHaan.com, addresses biblical Christianity to build a faith that matters.

Read his blog, receive his newsletter, and learn more at PeterDeHaan.com.

If you liked *That You May Know,* please leave a review online. Your review will help other people discover this book and encourage them to read it too. That would be amazing.

Thank you.

Books by Peter DeHaan

For the latest list of all Peter's books, go to PeterDe-Haan.com/books.

The Dear Theophilus series of devotional Bible studies:

> *That You May Know* (the gospel of Luke)
> *Tongues of Fire* (the book of Acts)
> *For Unto Us* (the prophet Isaiah)
> *Return to Me* (the Minor Prophets)
> *I Hope in Him* (the book of Job)
> *Living Water* (the gospel of John)
> *Love Is Patient* (Paul's letters to the Corinthians)

The 52 Churches series:

> *52 Churches*
> *The 52 Churches Workbook*
> *More Than 52 Churches*
> *The More Than 52 Churches Workbook*
> *Visiting Online Church*

The Bible Bios series:

>*Women of the Bible*
>*The Friends and Foes of Jesus*
>*Old Testament Sinners and Saints*

Other books:

>*Beyond Psalm 150*
>*Jesus's Broken Church*
>*Bridging the Sacred-Secular Divide*
>*Martin Luther's 95 Theses*
>*How Big Is Your Tent?*

Be the first to hear about Peter's new books and re-ceive updates at PeterDeHaan.com/updates.